MW00776557

MR. LUCKY

My Unexpected Journey to Success

Mitchell Epstein

© Mitchell Epstein 2019

Print ISBN: 978-1-54398-728-7
eBook ISBN: 978-1-54398-729-4

Some names have been changed to protect the privacy of individuals.
All rights reserved. This book or any portion thereof may not be reproduced or used in any manner whatsoever without the express written permission of the publisher except for the use of brief quotations in a book review.

Dedication Page

This book is dedicated to the two most important people in my life, Dawn and Melanie, and the two people whose lives have most influenced mine in the last few years, Coy and Jeron.

TABLE OF CONTENTS

INTRODUCTION

Mr. Lucky

My nickname when I was on the seventh-grade basketball team was Jelly. In college, some friends called me Big Mitch and others Mitchell A. Even now, they still do. In West Virginia, a client called me Einstein.

A couple of years ago, I randomly started calling myself Mr. Lucky. Why? I was just feeling good about things and starting to become more aware about life, rather than just living it. I kinda liked the sound of it. I didn't mention the name to anyone except my wife until I started writing this book. I never imagined that I would write a book, let alone a book about my life. I'm a pretty quiet, reserved person, and the last thing I ever want is to be the center of attention. The thought of sharing not just stories about my life, but many of my private thoughts almost stopped me from writing altogether.

But I like to help people. I always have, even though I was never conscious of it. When I think about this now I am somewhat surprised, since my attitude has generally been that we're all responsible for ourselves. If you want something, just do it, I would say. Figure it out and make it happen. I hadn't thought about how, for many people, that is easier said than done. I definitely haven't always been the most compassionate person in the world.

Take, for example, the most ordinary lucky day of my life: December 2, 1985. I was in south Florida on a business trip when I realized that "Da Bears"

– the 12-0 Chicago Bears – were playing a Monday night game against the Miami Dolphins. The Dolphins were trying to protect their legacy as the only undefeated NFL team in the modern era. Every player from the Dolphins' 1974 undefeated team would be at the game, and every diehard sports fan, myself included, wanted to be there as well.

I *had* to go to that game; but I didn't have a ticket. I called my dad to see if he could help. Nope. He told me he was going to the game with a buddy of his and wished me good luck. In those pre-cellphone days, he gave me his section, row, and seat number, hoping that at some point we would meet up.

I went to the stadium, knowing that with a yearly salary of barely over $20,000, this would be one of the toughest tickets I had ever scored in my young life. Although I had always managed to find a ticket, I was having no luck that night. I tried everything and nothing was working. And then I looked down, and what do you think I saw on the ground? Yes: a ticket to one of the most-hyped Monday night football games of all time. Now *mine*.

Exuberant, I entered the stadium and found my dad. He was shocked but very excited to see me. After I told him how lucky I'd been to find the ticket, he told me that his friend would be a little late to the game. Amazingly, his friend never made it so I actually got to sit with my dad the whole time while we watched the Dolphins win 38-24 in a game that ESPN ranks as the third-best Monday night game ever. My dad and I had been to at least a hundred sports events together – including the 1979 Super Bowl where the Steelers beat the Cowboys 35-31 because Jackie Smith dropped a perfect pass in the end zone from Roger Staubach – but this game was truly special.

Only recently, though, did someone point out to me that my spectacular luck on that day was due to someone else's misfortune. Wow, I never once considered that. Oblivion at best; at worst, a failure of compassion. I can only hope that the person who lost that ticket was able to convince the box office they had purchased it and was allowed to take their seat – because it would then be their luck that I wasn't in it, due to the absence of my father's friend.

And so the universe arranges itself, doling out the good fortune and miseries, not always in equal measure, but always mysteriously. Most important, I have learned we all have a choice in how we view the cards we are dealt and how we play them.

Ironically, compassion or no, I have been successful helping people, both personally and professionally. I now recognize that I am very happy when I am helping others and feel tremendous satisfaction and pride after doing so. In business, I was able to help organizations grow faster and more profitably, and fortunately I was able to make a good living at the same time. In the end, there was even a big payday.

During the last few years, I have been mentoring two terrific young men who were both homeless shortly before I met them. They were part of a program that provided reduced-cost housing and required them to be full-time college students and work full time simultaneously. I have been privileged to be part of their lives and to have them in mine. We have helped each other to be better than any of us thought we could be.

In each case we started out slowly, getting to know one another. I didn't know it at the time, but came to understand that both of them had seen many people come and go in their lives; in particular, their fathers. They were cautiously assessing how much they wanted to share with me, and in some ways I was doing the same. Gradually the conversations grew deeper, until now we talk about everything.

Later they told me how amazed they were that every week they would get that text from me, asking if this time or that was a good time to get together. I didn't realize how much they valued that I just showed up. I listened, I genuinely cared, I asked questions, I made suggestions. They probably didn't know how happy I was to spend time with them and how much joy I got hearing about what they were doing and accomplishing. I am proud to say that one of them is a successful realtor, who graduated with an MBA and at age twenty-three bought his own home. The other young man is equally phenomenal. He is a senior in college, working two jobs that fall on opposite ends of the social spectrum – one at a luxury hotel and the other at a foster care agency. Both young men are focused on giving back to our community.

Watching these men flourish has been so joyful and fulfilling that I wanted to do more. As I tried to figure out how I could help more than one or two people at a time, I made the decision to write this book. The name Mr. Lucky isn't intended to describe my life. I don't feel lucky that I had a very successful business; I feel fortunate. Like most successful entrepreneurs, I had a little luck along the way, but despite my self-bestowed nickname, I attribute very little of my success to luck.

Thomas A. Edison's statement best describes what I believe were the keys to my success: "The three great essentials to achieve anything worthwhile are: hard work, stick-to-itiveness, and common sense." You can't teach common sense, so I will try to inspire you with stories about work ethic; entertain you with my persistence; and educate you with simple but powerful ideas.

In case you think my life has been a bed of roses: Clearly there is nothing lucky about having your house burn down or your dad die of cancer or any number of the heartbreaking and challenging stories about my life that I will share. But in almost all of these cases, I considered myself extremely lucky because things could have turned out a lot worse. For now, let's just say that if I were a cat, I would definitely be running out of lives.

I have never been the smartest guy in the room, not even close. As you read my book I'll prove it to you over and over again! However, whether you are the smartest person in the room or someone like me, always willing to work hard and continually focused on making things better, I believe that the lessons I share in this book will help you to be more successful in your career and happier in your personal relationships and life. That, of course, is the ultimate success. I say this being, well, lucky enough to have had success both personally and professionally.

My hope is that I can inspire you with a story that has a less than auspicious start. My SAT score was 600 on the quantitative portion and 450 on the verbal section. Thankfully, I was accepted into the University of Florida in the fall of 1978 because my dad was a resident of Florida and the school hadn't become super-competitive yet. My grade point average in the second quarter was point nine. And no, that's not a typo: .9 percent – basically the equivalent of a D. Also, when I finished graduate school I interviewed with, and got rejection letters from, at least twenty-seven companies (yes, companies sent out letters back then).

When I was hired by the Federal Reserve Bank of Atlanta in May of 1984 as a Bank Examiner after getting my MBA, I am fairly certain my salary of $18,500 put me in the bottom 10 percent of my class. I may even have been the lowest-paid graduate from my MBA program.

Not the fastest start, but I did bounce back from that very, very fun second quarter of freshman year and graduated from the business school with honors in four years, and then earned an MBA in Finance from UF.

If that hasn't inspired you, hopefully this will. From 2000 to 2007 I not only experienced and survived enough tragedy for an entire lifetime, but I had more professional success than I ever dreamed possible. First, the tough parts: My mother-in-law was diagnosed with cancer at age sixty-one and died in less than a month. Three years later my house burned down, and my wife, daughter, and I lost 85 percent of our belongings. The following year my dad died of cancer at sixty-seven. Then we found out for ourselves that there is absolutely no factual basis in the theory that bad things happen in threes, when my talented, brilliant, and funny brother-in-law committed suicide three years later.

While many people would have found these challenges overwhelming, I am proud to say that during that same eight years I started a business, successfully grew and sold it for a lot of money, and retired at forty-seven years of age. All of this is secondary to the fact that I married my best friend twenty-nine years ago; my wife Dawn and I have a wonderful daughter whom we adopted twenty-four years ago; and today we are happier than ever.

As a fifty-nine-year-old man who thinks he is going to live for another forty years, I know how crucial it is to have a purpose. For me, it's helping others, and nothing makes me feel better. Fortunately, I've spent the majority of my career as a consultant so I had the chance to help others virtually every day. Mentoring has given me an even greater, more meaningful opportunity to contribute to society.

Over ten years have passed since I retired, which has provided me the opportunity to reflect on my life. On one hand there is a whole lot I would do differently. On the other hand, I am now beginning to understand that it's the tough times and the challenges that shape who we are and provide opportunities for growth.

I have come to realize that we have all faced many difficult situations, and how you deal with the tough stuff that life throws at you is crucial. I don't let these situations drag me down. No matter how bad they seem at the time, I immediately pick myself up and keep on going. In the past I have done this automatically and unconsciously by taking action, usually before I have even felt what really happened. Once the grief or challenge begins to sink in, I am already moving forward. Persist first; come to see the positive side as it reveals itself, even if it takes a while.

I have recently begun to figure out that "stuff" is always going to be heading our way. Sometimes it's gonna be big stuff, but more often it will be little nothings, testing us to see if we truly understand what's important. We always have a choice as to how we perceive every situation and how we react. Was my house burning down the worst thing that ever happened or was I the luckiest guy in the world? That's easy – classic Mr. Lucky – as my family and I are not only alive, but I have life lessons to share from this and so many challenging experiences.

In fact, we are all, or all can be, Mr. or Ms. Lucky. I now understand that Mr. Lucky is not a person but a worldview, one that I have learned to appreciate as I reflect on my life. We can all consciously practice counting our blessings rather than bemoaning our misfortunes – and in so doing, increase our joy in life.

I talk a lot about my work history in this book. Certainly anyone who is starting or building a business, thinking about customer service or marketing, or just working a job will find useful advice here. While you may be tempted to view some of the stories I tell as a business memoir, the lessons I convey from my professional experiences have universal applications as well.

In one I will describe how I turned "the stupidest idea I ever heard" into the foundation of the business I sold for millions. In another I will share a common-sense sales strategy that most business people will pooh-pooh. This simple idea will make your life better and your business much more profitable.

The other lessons reveal the lifelong benefits we can all derive from experiences we've had, if we learn to think about them differently. As you read and reflect, I hope you will try reframing some of the experiences you habitually think of as negative in your life to focus on the positive you can derive from them – the wisdom, strength, resilience, or compassion you have gained; the people you have met; the wonder of it all.

Cumulatively, the Mr. Lucky experiences I write about here add up to a philosophy or even a spiritual practice of "how to be." In short, this book is about how to build a life – a rich, satisfying life – from whatever circum-stances you may face. Hopefully, what I have learned and will share will help us all handle whatever comes our way with more love, compassion, and grace, for ourselves, our loved ones, and for the world around us.

And so in this spirit I offer this book. We all have a story to tell, and I hope that reading mine will help make some of your challenges a little more manageable, and your successes even sweeter. Most importantly, I hope I can give you the knowledge and courage to believe that you have everything you need to make your dreams come true – and to find your inner Mr. Lucky.

CHAPTER 1

My Dad

I hardly know where to start when I talk about my dad, but talking about him seems like a good place to begin my book, because so many of my life lessons involved my father. The "old goat," an affectionate name that I believe my sister, Lisa, coined after Dad died, had a big heart, and we shared more awesome times than I can recount. He was the best man at my wedding and probably my biggest fan and supporter in life after my wife.

I often wish that he could have been alive for my daughter's Bat Mitzvah, for the day I sold my company, to spend time with us in our beautiful home in Florida, or to drink a bottle of his favorite wine, Shafer Hillside Select, together. Most of all I wish I could see the smile on his face as he shared in the lives of his children, his grandchildren, and his nieces and nephews. I especially miss talking with him about almost every aspect of our lives. We spoke most days while he was living, and whether we agreed or disagreed, we always respected one another's opinion.

I'm incredibly thankful and appreciative for his love, all the good times we had, and the lessons I learned from him. From my perspective, my dad made many awful decisions, and I probably learned the most from those. I think his worst decision was moving from New York to Florida with his new wife and her daughter when I was fourteen and my sister was ten. I can't begin to understand how a man who believed so much in family could pick up and leave at such a crucial time in our lives. Surprisingly, we never talked about his decision to move.

Roughly two years prior, my parents got divorced. They never fought in front of us, and neither my sister nor I had any idea that my parents were having difficulties. When they called us into the living room to tell us the big news, we thought they were going to tell us that they were going on vacation and that we would be staying with our grandparents.

When my dad moved in 1994, long-distance telephone calls were a dollar a minute. Given the cost, a lot of our communication would occur through cassette tapes. On the way to or from work, my dad would talk to my sister and me about what was going on in his life by speaking into a cassette recorder, and he would then send one or more tapes to us. An envelope would arrive a few days or a week later with the word "Fragile" written on it. Most of the time we would listen to the tapes and then send them back after recording over them.

I'll give my dad points for creativity and his commitment to consistently sending the tapes. Then I have to quickly ask, "Dad, what were you thinking when you decided to move 1,287 miles away from your two kids?"

My sister and I would go to Florida during school vacations for a week or ten days at a time, three or four times a year, to see my dad, who was living with his new wife, Betty, and her daughter, Tracy. You can imagine if you only saw your teenage children a few times a year, these visits would be focused on them and you would probably try to do things that the kids would enjoy.

My dad definitely tried his best and usually these visits would start out well, as we were all excited to see one another. In my dad's effort to pack two or three months' worth of family time together with his kids into a week or so, he probably wasn't as sensitive to his wife or focused on her needs.

I am not exaggerating when I say that each time we visited, sooner or later there would be a blowup and our trip was ruined. My dad would try to patch things up. If the trigger was something I did, I would apologize. But once Betty got upset, she wasn't the type to quickly bounce back. Her energy was almost always very heavy and negative. Neither my sister nor I was used to being in a house with someone so loud and moody, and we were never able to adjust to her personality.

Emotions Matter

The saying "happy wife, happy life" captures what was wrong with Dad's life once he remarried, as his new wife was rarely happy except when she was on vacation. He prided himself on his ability to tune out all that was wrong, particularly between the two of them. This may have been easy for him, but it was brutal for my sister and me.

One thing I have learned since he died is that living your life surrounded by someone with such negative energy is not only draining, but extremely toxic and unhealthy. I think the emotional stress and other ramifications of living with her were among the factors leading to his cancer and ultimately to the melanoma that metastasized to his brain, causing his death at only sixty-seven years old.

Some people say that every day they think about the important people in their lives who have passed away. I don't think about my dad that often, and sometimes I wonder if it's because I never really processed his death. I don't remember if I took two or three days off when he died, but I know for sure that it wasn't a week. I "warriored" on, rationalizing that he would want to make sure that nothing – particularly him – slowed down my business.

I'm not sure if there is such a word as "warriored," but as my wife and daughter would attest, I like to make up words. I'm not sure why, except that it always seems like fun. My wife tells me all the time that life is about laughing more, having more fun, and being happy. And she is right. I would add that our purpose in life is also to make the world a better place.

I now recognize that when my dad died, I did the same unhealthy thing I had done too often in my life, which was to gloss over something painful. As a man, I know that I am not alone in doing this. I have observed that many men aren't good at dealing with their emotions, and I imagine it is extremely frustrating to the people around us. In fact, I know it is, because my wife has told me so. Getting more "in touch with my feelings" is something that I have worked on, and continue to do, and I am glad as it has deepened my relationship with Dawn.

I have a long way to go on this essential aspect of my life, but I am making significant progress, especially since I did not start working on this until I was forty-eight years old. For a long time I have believed you should try to improve some aspect of your life every day, or at the very least, each week. If you aren't always doing something to help others or yourself, you are wasting your life. For most of my life, I concentrated on improvements in business and finance. Now I'm focused on becoming a better person and helping others achieve their goals and dreams. In hindsight, I wish I had lived a more balanced life and I frequently recommend this to others, especially younger people.

Life Lessons from Mr. Lucky

Parenting is not optional – be there for your kids.

Emotional energy is powerful.

Learn to deal with your emotions.

Try to improve some aspect of your life – or someone else's life – every day or week.

Strive to lead a more balanced life.

CHAPTER 2
College Days

The story of how I went from a .9 grade point average (GPA) in my second quarter at the University of Florida to graduating with honors is pretty straightforward. First, there was the brutally frank discussion/chewing out from my dad. He and Mom had talked and this was one situation in which they were in total agreement. They were fairly certain that I wasn't taking school seriously and that I was capable of doing much better.

When I asked my mom about this recently, she said their message was simple. "You had one quarter to straighten up or we were done paying for college or anything else for that matter. As far as we were concerned, you could party all you wanted and be a bum, but we weren't planning on footing that bill."

There wasn't much I could say in my defense, and there was no way I could look at either of them with a straight face and say that I was trying. The fact is I couldn't look at anyone with a straight face back then, as I was usually stoned and had been since ninth grade. In high school, my friends and I had a simple rule. If we were in the car long enough to fill a bowl, we would get high.

College started out in a similar manner, and I could tell an endless number of fun and entertaining stories about those days. However, the reality is that we did lots of unbelievably stupid and dangerous stuff. Thankfully I figured things out before it cost me my college career or my life. The turn-around wasn't quick or complete, although I almost tripled my GPA the next quarter. That rare achievement still only resulted in a 2.5 GPA.

My summer job at Citibank helped cement the message that I needed to get my act together. All I did for eight hours each day was take travelers checks out of a box and compare the numbers on the checks to a piece of paper in the box to make sure the numbers matched. This may have been the most boring job in America.

What drove the message home was that about fifteen grown men traveled an hour or two each way for this job. The most exciting aspect of the day occurred first thing in the morning and after lunch if you were the person whose turn it was to choose the radio station that we would all listen to for the next four hours. As an intern I was not included in the rotation, and they never chose a station that played the Allman Brothers or the Grateful Dead. This was one summer job that I definitely did not want to turn into a career.

From that point onward my grades were very good and I believe I made an A in every economics class (my major in the business school). In hindsight, I wish someone had sat down with me and put school in perspective: Go to class and study. The typical workday in the real world is forty hours, and many people work a whole lot more. In college the average class load is fifteen hours a week. If you study an additional fifteen to thirty hours, almost anybody with average intelligence will do reasonably well. Unless you are also working fulltime, that still leaves a lot of time to have fun. For me, nothing was more fun than going to Gator football and basketball games with my friends.

Besides academics, one of the most valuable things I did during college was join the coed business fraternity, Delta Sigma Pi, where I made some lifelong friends. The Beta Eta chapter at UF met Thursday nights, and we often had business leaders speak at our meetings. I become the Chancellor of our fraternity, which meant I had to learn Robert's Rules of Order, parliamentary procedure, so I could run the meetings efficiently and effectively. This was an important skill that helped me tremendously throughout each stage of my business career.

Life Lessons from Mr. Lucky

Go to class.

Have fun but study.

CHAPTER 3
Early Career

I'm not sure exactly why I moved to Atlanta after graduation. I like to joke that it was because I had family in New York and Florida and college friends in Atlanta. The truth probably was that the Federal Reserve Bank of Atlanta offered me a job as a bank examiner.

You don't get paid a lot when you work for a government agency (technically, the Fed is a quasi-government agency), but the job was great. I learned a lot about banking quickly, as the bank exams we performed were one to three weeks long. Even more significant, my boss gave me a lot of responsibility.

The exams were divided into two parts. The first and most critical part, lending, examined the quality of the bank's loan portfolio. The second part evaluated the operations of the bank, including liquidity and interest rate risk management. Within six months I was leading the operations review and presenting the operating deficiencies to the executive management team of each bank at the end of their exam.

I enjoyed the liquidity management aspect of the job, as this involved reviewing the investment portfolio of the bank. Interest rate risk management (IRRM) was my favorite and, as it turned out, this positioned me well for my next job. In simple terms, IRRM involves understanding what happens to a bank's earnings and value due to fluctuations in interest rates.

A little background information will help you understand how perfect my timing was in learning about IRRM. It was a relatively new discipline in banking that came to the forefront as a result of interest rates spiking in the late 1970s. The prime rate (currently 5.5 percent) increased from 9 percent on July 30, 1978 to 21.5 percent on December 19, 1980. Home mortgage rates (currently about 4.00 percent) peaked at 18.45 percent in October of 1981 and the Fed funds rate spiked to 20 percent (currently 2.5 percent). Deregulation of interest rates on some bank deposits also occurred in the early 1980s.

The surge and deregulation of interest rates caused huge economic problems including the Savings & Loan (S&L) crisis, which resulted in 1,043 out of 3,234 institutions failing. When rates increased so dramatically, their net interest spread – basically the difference between deposit rates and loan rates – went from roughly 300 basis points to extremely negative.

The crisis was made worse as the government failed to close these institutions and instead allowed them to enter high-risk areas of banking. Not only did the S&Ls lack the needed expertise, their regulators were equally ill-prepared to deal with the greater complexity of the new lines of business. The situation was further exacerbated by massive amounts of fraud.

They say timing in life is everything, and in my case learning about, and focusing on, interest rate risk management right after this tumultuous period was very significant for two reasons. First, people with years of experience in banking had no more knowledge in this discipline than I did. From this time forward banks would obsess about, and fear, interest rates spiking. In my next job I would not only help clients manage through this issue, I would also be able to help them dramatically increase their earnings. As a result, they liked me a lot!

Learn to Write

As I think back about my days at the Fed, I am appreciative of the structure that went into preparing the examination reports. Each report was examined by the review department. They had to be factually accurate and grammatically correct. While I never developed the writing skills of an attorney, between graduate school and the Fed, I turned into a pretty good writer.

To this day I am amazed at the poor communication skills of so many college graduates. I hate to sound like an old man, but I don't think texting and Twitter are helping advance the writing skills of today's youth. I strongly encourage everyone to work on their communication skills, primarily public speaking and writing. This will pay off in virtually all aspects of life.

My time at the Fed was valuable for many reasons but none more so than making lifelong friends, including my best friend for many years, Courtney Dufries. Courtney was one of the people involved in my interview process, playing a peer-to-peer role, as he had only been with the Fed for a year himself and was also twenty-four years old. We were both huge Allman Brothers fans and we hit it off immediately.

The Fed was full of quirky people, and my team became like a second family as we traveled the southeast region two or three weeks a month. Meals were always entertaining; we had liberals like Courtney and good ole country boys like my friend Henry Chandler White III (Chan). I think the only thing they agreed upon was drinking Jack Daniels and that the three of us should go out together a couple of nights a week to make some new friends. Nothing was more entertaining than watching Chan tell stories to pretty young ladies.

The Fed was a fantastic place to start my career, but after three years I was ready to move on. I had learned a lot about asset liability management (ALM) and had a strong lending foundation. When the head of the department conducted my exit interview, I told him that their salary structure wasn't designed for ambitious people like me. I was always rated outstanding, and the difference between my raise and someone rated average wasn't enough to buy a six-pack of imported beer. (Yes, back then it was either Jack-and-ginger or a Heineken.)

Looking back fondly at my days as a G-man, I think the most meaningful lesson I learned is that your first couple of jobs shouldn't just be about the money. It's all about gaining experience. Your boss and the quality and reputation of the company you work for should be given as much consideration as your salary. I'm not going to say money isn't important, because it certainly is, but money will not make you happy.

You have a lot better chance of being happy and successful in life if you enjoy your work. If you do want to compete with others based on money, recognize that it's the skills and experience from your first jobs, not your salary, that will give you the best chance of winning in the long run. That was definitely my experience.

Life Lessons from Mr. Lucky

Enhance your communications skills.

Use your first jobs to gain skills and experience.

Focus on experience before money.

Find work you enjoy and feel is meaningful.

CHAPTER 4
First Nationwide Network

O ne Friday night in the spring of 1987, I ran into Jane Doyle, a former Fed employee, at happy hour. Jane had left the Fed about a year earlier to work for a consulting company called First Nationwide Network (FNN). As we talked, FNN sounded like an interesting place to work so I asked her to let me know if something in asset liability management (ALM) opened up there. Fortunately, something came available almost immediately.

FNN was a nationwide bank consulting company with roughly fifty employees, located in Atlanta. Most of their clients were relatively small banks and savings and loans institutions (S&Ls). FNN hired me in their ALM area, which primarily focused on liquidity and interest rate risk management.

My boss and I traveled to institutions to help them improve their ALM process. We also trained some banks on Sendero's ALM software, which allowed them to simulate the impact that a change in interest rates would have on earnings and their capital position.

My boss got fired about ninety days after I took the job. Since ALM was somewhat of a niche area and was certainly not considered vital, they didn't replace him, and I was the lone remaining member of the department. In some ways this was far from ideal, as we had only gone out on the road a few times together and I was relatively young, twenty-seven years old, and inexperienced. But this was also an excellent opportunity if I could figure things out quickly and keep our clients happy.

The following month I went to Sendero's annual conference in Scottsdale, Arizona, which I found fascinating. I distinctly remember a presenter discussing a number of strategies that were counter to traditional banking beliefs. The Sendero software could be utilized to model and test these strategies.

When I started in ALM, most banks that purchased the Sendero model or hired FNN for ALM consulting did so to check a regulatory box, not because they thought this was a critical initiative. What I quickly learned from attending conferences and from training our clients was that this software generated very valuable information. After spending a couple of days training a client to use the software, the two of us would know as much about the bank's balance sheet as anyone else at the bank. Understanding the balance sheet provided powerful insight into how the bank made money. We could then use the software to test the impact that alternative strategies would have on the bank's earnings; very often the impact was dramatic.

Figure Out What Is Important

A bank's ALM Committee (ALCO) typically included the top five people at the bank. Given the composition of the ALCO, it had the potential to be an important committee, if not the most important. However, because the few key pages of analysis the software generated were lumped in with so much worthless information, most of the time the committee glossed over it. In addition to interest rate risk, this committee was also responsible for managing liquidity risk. As essential as risk management is, the ALCO was regarded as so boring that people would do whatever they could to avoid going to the meeting.

What I needed to do was figure out why this potentially powerful committee added little to no value. I quickly concluded that while risk management is an absolutely essential part of any business, the purpose of a for-profit organization is to provide value to its customers in a way that increases shareholder value. For a bank, this primarily means making more money in both the short run and long run. In order for any business to accomplish this, it must manage its risks; banks are no different in this regard.

Based on this logic, I questioned why *all* banks had ALCOs (risk management committees) and *no* banks had profitability committees. I believed that instead of having a committee that focused on risk, banks should have a committee that focused on profitability, with responsibility to manage the risks associated with achieving the profitability objectives.

Given this new, more meaningful objective of increasing profitability, I focused on revamping the ALCO meeting agenda, the pre-meeting package, and the committee's emphasis. I wanted to make it a meeting people would be eager to attend and to give the participants the most actionable information in the least number of pages possible.

I recommended structuring the meeting around each major discipline that impacted profitability. As time went on and I participated in more ALCO meetings, I recognized that the loan and deposit pricing process at banks was unsophisticated and overly influenced by the local competition. Eventually I determined that not only was pricing the most consequential factor in banking, it provided the greatest opportunity for value creation. This realization would be the basis for the company I started ten years later, which focused entirely on loan and deposit pricing.

Make Things Simple

People have a tendency to make things more complicated than necessary, and that's also true of banking. Let me try to make banking as simple as possible:

One of the main things that a bank does is take in money from one group of people: depositors, and provide that money to another group: borrowers. The bank is the middleman, guaranteeing the depositor that they will have access to their money either immediately or at a specific time. Depending on the type of deposit, the bank will pay interest to the depositor. The bank charges the borrower based on the loan characteristics such as purpose, maturity, repricing, collateral, and risk. The bank's objective is to make money from this process.

There are more qualified people wanting to borrow money when the economy is strong, creating more competition for deposits. Fortunately for banks, in particular community banks, in the 1990s the Federal Home Loan Bank (FHLB) started offering them the opportunity to borrow money. So instead of only getting money from depositors, the bank could pick and choose where they got money based on the interest cost. This presented a fantastic opportunity to help control a bank's interest expense, and in the 1990s interest expense was a community bank's largest expense.

Challenge the Conventional Wisdom

Many banks told me they did not want to take advantage of this great opportunity. The two biggest reasons given were that "Banks don't borrow money" and that "We are a relationship bank." The first assertion is preposterous and the second sounds good on the surface but is equally flawed.

The statement that banks don't borrow money implies that there is something wrong with borrowing money. Yet banks lend money to individuals and businesses all day long, and lending is the most crucial activity for community banks. So what is wrong with borrowing money? I would also carefully make a lengthy case that there was virtually no difference between a deposit (someone else's money) and borrowed money.

The second part of the discussion regarding relationships is interesting because the simple statement about their importance is frequently used to justify bad decisions. Everyone would quickly agree that if the cost was the same, getting money locally was better.

In reality, the cost of raising new money from the local market was often dramatically higher than borrowing money from the FHLB. When I would point this out, people defended the additional expense based on the idea that relationships are valuable. I would always ask our client if they tracked the new business generated from a promotion or special so that I could review the impact and validate the assumption. Ninety-five percent of the time they didn't, and when they did, the results were always the same. The banks rarely attracted new customers from a promotion; instead they ended up paying their existing customers a lot more than necessary. The reality was that hardly anyone was willing to move their primary checking account under almost any circumstance.

Similar situations occur on the loan side. A lender would rationalize giving a low rate to a borrower because of how influential the borrower was, with the expectation that the person or entity would help the bank get additional business. In those infrequent situations when they did help bring in business, their friends were well aware of how favorable the terms were and they expected the same.

Tracking and monitoring critical information is essential for making high quality decisions in every industry. Businesses need their employees to challenge the rationales that are used to justify decisions. The failure to do so negatively impacted earnings at most banks that I consulted with. Fortunately this presented an opportunity for me to look at things with a fresh perspective and enabled me to show them ways to make a lot more money with little or no additional risk.

Life Lessons from Mr. Lucky

Take advantage of every opportunity.

Less is often more.

Look for opportunities to reframe situations to create and increase value.

Make things as simple as possible.

Don't be afraid to challenge conventional wisdom.

CHAPTER 5
Adoption

L ife's challenges often come with valuable lessons – and thankfully sometimes with fantastic endings. It's easy to take for granted the process of
having a baby, and then one day a doctor tells you the probability of having
a baby through the normal fun way of getting pregnant is minimal. This is
stressful and shocking but you quickly learn that about 10 percent of couples
face this challenge, and there are options available if you really want a child.

Even though it felt like it at first, it definitely wasn't the end of the world.
This unexpected hurdle gave us time to more fully consider the enormous
responsibility of parenting and to envision our life with and without children. After much discussion we decided that we definitely wanted a child.
Dawn and I spent a little over a year going through infertility treatment
with tremendous disappointment and frustration before we started down
the adoption path.

Adoption can also be difficult, expensive, time-consuming, and frankly,
somewhat of a crapshoot. Even though I wanted to have children, I worried
about how I would feel about an adopted child. Then I realized that I had
a dog I loved. If I could love an animal, why wouldn't I love a baby just
because it wasn't our biological child? This helped, but I was still concerned
about the specifics of the parents. What if our child was born to someone

who abused alcohol or drugs? I was also uncomfortable with the idea of raising a child with Down syndrome or some other significant health issue. I recognize that this wasn't 100 percent rational, as we could have had a baby who had complications if we had conceived the traditional way. But given a choice, I wanted a healthy baby.

The more we learned, the more we developed a strong preference for a newborn baby, and we desired an open adoption if possible. We believed that knowing who the birthparents were would be a real advantage for our child. He or she would have valuable medical or genetic information. More importantly, our child would never have to search for his or her birth parents, and we hoped that he or she would be able to meet these people in a controlled setting. We were also concerned that children who have never seen or met their birth parents tend to romanticize or fantasize about them, mainly during challenging times.

Fortunately we were able to arrange for an open adoption, and when it comes to my daughter's birth mother, Michelle, we could not have been luckier. She has been totally respectful of the relationship and supportive of us as parents. Dawn recently reminded me of the one time the open adoption turned a little tricky. Michelle typically sent a letter to either our daughter, Melanie, or all three of us every year. The letter she sent when Mel was ten informed us that she had had a baby. Melanie was so excited to have a sister that she told Dawn she would be going to live with them. Melanie added that she would "really miss my friends…. and you guys." Dawn calmly informed her that she was "stuck with us" but we would be happy to take her to visit Michelle and her half-sister.

The story of how we ended up with Mel is nothing short of a miracle. The most common way to adopt a baby born in the U.S. is through an adoption agency. Prospective couples looking to adopt put together a book that will provide birth mothers the opportunity to get to know them. (Although I don't have any experience with online dating, I imagine this might be like using Match.com.) If you're lucky, when the birth mother narrows down her search, you will be one of the couples she wants to interview. This process is something like trying to get into a highly competitive school. Lots of kids want to go to an Ivy League college, yet no one is exactly sure what the admission requirements are, so they hope for the best.

We went to an adoption conference and learned that networking is another way of finding a child. We ended up hiring the lawyer who spoke about this at the event, Ruth Claiborne. She recommended telling everybody we knew or encountered that we were looking to adopt a baby. When we sent out our holiday card, we asked family and friends to spread the word. We were also told that it was a waste of time to say anything to attorneys, as they would likely pass information about a baby available for adoption to someone in the business or their own client.

In addition to networking, we decided to interview adoption agencies to increase our chances and had a meeting set up for early January. In the meantime, we began working on our adoption book for prospective birth mothers. One day in December, Dawn was making copies of an early draft and her administrative assistant optimistically said, "Wouldn't it be great if you got a baby for Christmas?" Dawn said that realistically, we hoped we would by the following Christmas.

A few days later, on December 26th, we got a call from my very excited father and my stepmother, who had ignored the part about not telling attorneys that we were looking to adopt. My father's good friend, an attorney, had a fifteen-year-old niece who had given birth prematurely, on December 24th, to a three-pound-six-ounce baby girl. The birth mother and her family, all Jewish, were excited to find a couple who seemed so perfect.

The next forty-eight hours were an emotional roller coaster. We immediately called Ruth who said that the situation didn't sound promising due to concerns about the health of a premature baby, but that she would call the hospital to get the details. While we were waiting to hear back, we called my mother. She made our attorney sound like an optimist as she shared every horror story you could imagine about the health issues of a baby born seven or eight weeks early. She urged us to run away from this situation.

Ruth called back quickly to tell us that things appeared much more favorable than expected. Although the baby had been born early, she had been able to breathe without going on a ventilator and she was eating. We were ecstatic!

What now? For starters, we lived in Atlanta and the baby was born in Kissimmee, Florida. More importantly, we didn't have an agency to facilitate the adoption, which was a Florida requirement, and we hadn't started on a home study that is required of all adoptive parents.

Ruth recommended that we go to Florida as quickly as possible to meet the baby and the birth mother. We thought this was ideal, as we wanted to begin bonding with the baby immediately. First thing the next morning, we went to get fingerprinted as part of the home study process to determine our capability for being good parents. We stopped at a bookstore to get a book of baby names and then we hit the road for our seven-hour drive to Kissimmee.

We could not have been more excited and nervous. Even the idea of choosing a name caused anxiety. So many names reminded one of us of someone we had already met in our life with whom we associated something negative. We focused on names that honored Dawn's grandparents, Murray and Gertie, who had already passed on, and managed to agree on Melanie Grace just before we arrived. Later we found a Hebrew name to honor my grandpa Harry.

The next stop was our hotel, where we had a quick meeting with Michelle, the birth mother, and her mom, Marsha. All I remember was that we were thirty-four years old and Marsha, the grandmother, was only two or three years older!

Dawn remembers how mature Michelle was. She assured us that she wanted only the best for the baby and she was pleased that we wanted Melanie to meet her at the right time. Michelle recently told me that once she met us, a weight was lifted. She knew at that stage in her life there was no way she could have provided Melanie the life she deserved. More importantly, she has never second-guessed her decision.

After the meeting we followed Marsha to the hospital and received permission to see Melanie. We stood behind a glass window and gazed into a room filled with babies. Melanie was in an incubator, tiny as could be, with one leg twisted around at an odd angle. We looked at her and looked at each other, wondering why nobody had mentioned this. My mind was racing back to all the nightmarish things my mother had warned us about. Fortunately, there was nothing wrong with Mel; she was just tiny, having shrunk down to three pounds.

The good thing about her weight was that she wouldn't be released from the hospital until she was four pounds, which would give us time to go through the home study and regulatory process before she could be released into our custody. If the red tape wasn't cleared up before Mel reached four pounds, she would be placed in a foster home temporarily.

The next thirty days were stressful but they were filled with joy as well. We were able to spend several hours a day at the hospital, holding Mel, feeding her, and rocking her to sleep. This was incredible. If you have never seen or held a three-pound baby, let me tell you, they are unbelievably tiny. I still remember being petrified, slapping this wee little thing on the back to help her burp after she drank from the bottle. When I say Dawn and I knew absolutely nothing about babies, I'm not exaggerating. Thankfully the nurses all came to love Mel and they taught us a lot.

A few days later Dawn and I spent a memorable, though nontraditional, New Year's Eve in Florida. First we went out for a casual dinner – Mexican food, if I remember correctly. Then we went to the hospital so we could be with the person whom we hoped would soon become our daughter. At midnight we had sparkling grape juice with Mel and the nurses, and the next day I flew home to Atlanta.

For the next month I would basically spend Thursday night to Monday morning with Dawn at the hospital and then go back to Atlanta or to a client's location for work. Dawn stayed at a hotel in Kissimmee except for the days that she had to be in Atlanta for the home study.

One of the more stressful things that occurred during that month was when Michelle came to the hospital. She wanted to hold Melanie before she signed the papers relinquishing her parental rights. Dawn held her breath the entire time, knowing that there would be nothing we could do if Michelle changed her mind.

We also hired a private investigator to find the birth father, as he also needed to sign the papers relinquishing his parental rights. A week or two later he was located and signed them. We have never met or spoken with him. With the documents signed, the last step was to finish the home study before Mel reached four pounds.

The adoption home study process was extremely thorough and at times somewhat intrusive. We felt lucky that we ended up with Laura as our case-worker. She helped turn this stressful process into a time of reflection and focus on our marriage and how essential parenting really is. Laura was so caring through this process that a couple of years later Dawn was inspired to become an adoption caseworker as a part-time career.

Miraculously, or possibly with a little help from the nurses, Mel gained the final ounce and weighed four pounds on the day our home study was complete. Since the State of Florida approval of the adoption would take a few more days, we were not allowed to cross the state line and take her home to Atlanta quite yet. I immediately flew back to Kissimmee, and Dawn and I took Melanie from the hospital.

Our first stop was Target, where we bought a car seat and a Pack 'n Play bassinet for our first night together. Dawn barely slept that night, as she was constantly checking to make sure Mel was breathing. Being the typical guy, I slept well. We spent the next few days at my mother's home in Boca Raton, Florida, where friends and family had the opportunity to meet Mel.

A few days later the state approved our adoption paperwork, and we headed home. Everywhere Dawn went people commented on how terrific she looked to have a newborn baby. We would just smile and say thanks. Dawn was so grateful that we finally had a baby that she did virtually all the middle-of-the-night feedings, and Mr. Lucky was able to sleep.

My now-twenty-four-year-old daughter is a very sweet, wonderful young lady of whom I am extremely proud. I am optimistic that our relationship will continue to grow and we will be able to enjoy each other even more, now that we have made it through the difficult teen and college years. I have learned so much through the process of being a father, including perhaps the toughest lesson of all: sometimes my daughter doesn't want my opinion and I'm better off biting my tongue.

I have such respect and appreciation for Melanie's birth mother. Michelle did one of the hardest things imaginable, bringing Mel into the world when she was so young and recognizing that everyone would be better off if she chose adoption. I can't state this strongly enough. She gave us the most meaningful gift of our lives: our daughter. I will be forever grateful for her and to her, and wish her nothing but the best as she goes through the rest of her life.

Life Lessons from Mr. Lucky

Find the silver lining, always.

Learn to bite your tongue.

CHAPTER 6

The Grass Isn't Always Greener

E ven though I enjoyed my job at FNN, there were a couple of times when I considered making a career change. I was a big fan of Starbucks, and when I was about thirty-three years old, I thought about opening a local coffee shop. I initially thought that this was a pretty straightforward, cool business. Thankfully, rather than make a rash decision about something so consequential, I talked with a number of people to get their perspective.

The biggest factor that helped me decide not to go in this direction were the hours. Specifically, I realized that opening up at 5:00 am or even 6:00 and working until at least 6:00 pm, six or seven days a week, was going to be brutal. I wasn't afraid of hard work, yet this seemed even less family-friendly than being a consultant and traveling three or four days a week. Given that Dawn and I were planning to start a family at that time, this alone was a deal killer.

I also thought about becoming a financial planner or stockbroker. I was excited about the idea of being a broker, as I always enjoyed following the financial markets. I discussed this option a lot with my dad, since he had been in the business for thirty-five years. We talked about working together, and he even indicated that he would probably turn over his book of business to me at some point.

Looking back on these alternatives, mostly the second one, I again recognize how lucky I have been. I relished the opportunity to work with my dad, but that was offset by the idea that if I did, I would almost certainly have to spend more time with my stepmother. I truly dodged a bullet, because my relationship with her went from very bad to even worse.

After twenty-plus years of frustration, disappointment, and anguish I told my father that, except in the rarest of circumstances, I never wanted to be in the same place as Betty. Because I was so close to my father, this was a terribly difficult decision. But I also recognized that life is about choices, and I didn't want to spend any more time with such a negative person.

Telling my dad that his wife was no longer welcome at our house and that we would never go to his house again if there was any chance of her being there was a big deal. The understanding that this was something we could do came from a seminar about infertility that Dawn and I had attended. The holidays were approaching, and the speakers talked about how difficult they are for people in general and then focused on how tough it is for those dealing with infertility.

One of the pieces of wisdom that was shared at this seminar was the reminder that we are adults and we have control of our lives. We have the ability to make decisions, even when these choices will disappoint others. They were advocating that some couples might be better off not attending upcoming holiday celebrations. This gave us the knowledge and the confidence that we didn't have to do anything we didn't want to. How empowering is that?

This is worth repeating: If you are an adult living on your own, you have complete control over your life and you never have to do anything you don't want to do. I am not saying that this is always easy, but remembering this is essential. I also think it's worth pointing out that this doesn't give you the right to be a jerk. In fact, I recommend the exact opposite. Our words and actions are powerful, and we can't take them back or undo them no matter how much we would like to. And believe me, there are so many instances where I wish I could.

I can't say this strongly enough: What we say and do usually has consequences, so it behooves us to be thoughtful, particularly in how we handle difficult situations. When the time came, we applied this lesson to give ourselves the right to not see my stepmother.

I talked with my father endlessly about his wife, wondering why he stayed in his marriage. "Money" was the best answer I ever got. When he had it, he wasn't willing to get divorced and split it with her. Then he lost it all anyway; go figure. On reflection, I think that he feared living alone.

But isn't living alone superior to living with someone who treats you badly and makes you unhappy? My mother taught me many valuable things. She taught me to be independent long before I went to college, including introducing me to the washer and dryer when I was twelve or thirteen. One of her more significant lessons was to learn to enjoy time by oneself. She believed that in a healthy relationship, both people should spend time with their friends and do things separately, and also feel free to spend time alone. After all, if you don't enjoy your own company, why would anyone else?

Life Lessons from Mr. Lucky

Take control and "just say no" to the negative people in your life.

Remember your words matter.

Learn to enjoy being by yourself.

CHAPTER 7
We Were Robbed

Every avid sports fan can recall a game or two where the referee made a bad call that robbed their team of the win, or that amazing play at the end of the game where the other team stole the game and broke your heart. For most Gator fans, that's the ninety-three-yard pass play from Buck Belue to Lindsay Scott in the Georgia Bulldogs' 26-21 last-minute win at the "World's Largest Outdoor Cocktail Party." Not only was that my first of many games in Jacksonville, but freshman running back Hershel Walker rushed for 238 yards and the Dogs won the National Championship that year.

That loss to the Dogs still stings – it's faithfully recounted each year when the two teams play – but an even worse memory is from a night when my buddy Courtney and I walked home from a Braves game. I knew this wasn't the smartest idea, as the neighborhood had a fairly high level of homeless people and drugs, but I told myself that I was with my tough Irish friend. We had gone to countless Braves and Falcons games together but had never taken this route.

We were about halfway back to Courtney's place when two youths with stockings over their heads jumped out in front of us. One of them had a silver gun. I'm not a gun guy but it seemed big enough and it was pointed directly at my crotch, inches away in fact. Courtney remembers them telling us to go into the woods and me answering, "No way." What I remember is being ordered to give them our money, so I gave them my wallet.

We were robbed. And just like that they turned away to leave. Holy smokes. I quickly regained some composure and shouted, "Take the money, leave the wallet." And then I shouted it one more time: "Take the money, leave the wallet."

Believe it or not, they left my wallet, which held my credit cards and driver's license. We walked over, grabbed it, and headed to Courtney's house as fast as we could for a shot of Jack Daniels – a few, actually. Mr. Lucky escaped with not only his wallet, but his watch, the ring that Dawn gave him for his thirtieth birthday, and *his life*.

I'm still not sure what life lesson was gained from that night. I certainly found out that Courtney wasn't the toughest guy in the neighborhood. He stood there quietly and did nothing; some tough guy he was. Maybe the lesson was to ask for what you want, no matter the circumstances.

I don't have nightmares about that night or think about it often, but I constantly look over my shoulder when I'm walking at night in a big city and even sometimes when I'm walking home alone after a late night listening to music in relatively safe Sarasota. I occasionally walk down the middle of the street or move from sidewalk to sidewalk when I find myself with that uncomfortable feeling. I know I should probably just grab an Uber late at night, but I love to get a few steps in before the sun rises.

Life Lessons from Mr. Lucky

Ask for what you want.

Trust and respect your intuition.

CHAPTER 8

"Stupidest Idea I Have Ever Heard" – Worth Millions

One of the things that helped me most in my business career was that I was always looking for ways to create additional value and I didn't care where they came from. One day I was in a meeting with Kurt, the EVP of USBA (the same company as FNN but they changed their ownership structure and name), and Gary, a consultant who worked for me for a couple of years.

Gary had created some Excel spreadsheets that we used during our consulting engagements and gave to our clients for their continued benefit. The clients loved the spreadsheets, as they helped their lenders develop pricing scenarios that were attractive to the borrower and profitable for the bank; a true win-win situation. Best of all, the spreadsheets were easy to use, so the lenders actually liked them.

The three of us were in a meeting when Kurt asked if we had considered licensing the spreadsheets. Gary immediately said that was the stupidest idea he had ever heard. He stated with 100 percent certainty that there was no way that a bank would ever license an Excel spreadsheet. Kurt thought we should try and the conversation quickly ended.

In hindsight, the stupidest idea that Gary ever heard may have been the single most valuable suggestion I ever received. When we finally converted the spreadsheets to "real software" four years later, we already had 200 banks licensing them. Perhaps most ironic was that Kurt and Gary were two of the most difficult people I worked with during my career.

Kurt epitomized everything that I despised in someone leading an organization. He had a gigantic ego and he lacked integrity. Gary brought a lot of value to my two-and-a-half-person department, as he was very intelligent. Unfortunately, he carried himself with an "I'm so smart" air about him and he was almost always in a sour mood.

Gary was probably a lot smarter than me, which may have contributed to his attitude, but fortunately I was his boss. I thought about Kurt's recommendation to license the spreadsheets. I knew that our clients wanted them and were getting tremendous benefit from them. I believed we had nothing to lose by asking our prospects to license the spreadsheets, so I met with our corporate attorney. We quickly put together a short licensing agreement and began including it in our consulting agreement. I think Gary found another job before we had ten licensed users.

Recurring Revenue – the Holy Grail

From then on, clients licensed our spreadsheets and were obligated to pay an annual fee if they wanted to continue using them. Recurring revenue in things like insurance, phone service, and cable have been around forever; however, it has become much more significant in the software industry in the last twenty years and is relatively limited in the consulting world.

We started out modestly, and the licensing fee for the first banks was only one or two thousand dollars. Over time, as we increased the functionality and expanded the capabilities, we increased the annual licensing charge. I also went back to the banks we had initially given them to and asked if they wanted to license them. Almost all of them did, which generated additional recurring revenue for us and provided them with the upgrades. We also benefited by reducing the number of banks that could turn around and give the spreadsheets away to others.

Look at Things from a Different Perspective

In all the times I have talked with people about my business, I don't think anybody has ever told me about another business where they licensed Excel spreadsheets. Of course, hindsight is 20-20, so we know Kurt was right and Gary was wrong.

So why did I implement a strategy of licensing Excel spreadsheets? I have been told I look at things differently than other people – that I frequently have a unique perspective or I am able to assess a situation and articulate a solution in a way others aren't. I'm not sure why that is, but as I stated at the beginning of the book, it's not because I'm the smartest guy in the room.

I think a better question than why did I implement a strategy of licensing Excel spreadsheets is why did Gary and so many other people think that they couldn't? My assessment was this: Our spreadsheets were simple to use and provided significant value. Why wouldn't someone license them if they were reasonably priced? If I had tried to charge more, maybe prospects would have balked. Fortunately they didn't, and this created tremendous value for my business.

Every idea isn't a good one, but don't let anyone quickly convince you that your idea, strategy, product, invention, or dream can't be achieved without looking at it fully and from different perspectives. One thing that made the licensing strategy attractive was that the downside was limited. We didn't have to do any market research or make an additional investment. We literally just had to ask our prospects to pay for something that had value to them.

I learned that one of my most valuable skills was the ability to simplify concepts that others found complex. Many times the concepts were elementary, but people just missed the big picture and made things more complicated than necessary. Other times, they simply got bogged down in the minutia.

There were also situations in which someone saw an opportunity or solution but they couldn't convince the group, and I could. I had a knack for taking these ideas and presenting them in a way that helped people recognize their importance. Whenever possible I tried to quantify the impact of an opportunity. I found that saying things like "big" or "a lot" didn't really get people's attention. Instead of saying "This will increase earnings a lot," I would say "This will increase earnings by approximately $100,000." Quantifying the impact allowed people to make their own decision about the importance.

As significant as having a good idea or product, the second and perhaps most critical aspect of success is best summarized by Nike's trademarked slogan: "Just do it." I have helped a lot of people and businesses by simply making sure that the "Most Important Stuff" actually gets done! I believe not being the smartest guy gives me an advantage, as I am rarely accused of making things too complicated. Instead, I always try to simplify things so that everyone understands exactly what needs to be done.

Before I move on I want to reiterate that a key factor that facilitated the creation of value in my business came from a discussion with two of the most challenging people in my career. In a world that has become increasingly polarized we are often placed in situations with people that have very different viewpoints. My consulting work necessitated that I listen extra carefully when those situations arose so that I fully understood alternative perspectives. Thankfully, I overcame the natural tendency to tune out Kurt and Gary.

In the last eighteen months, I have read two books that focus on decision making that I highly recommend. In Ray Dalio's fantastic book *Principles*, he spends multiple chapters describing his approach to making the best decisions personally and professionally. Dalio, the founder of one of the largest hedge funds, Bridgewater Capital, and the sixty-seventh richest man in the world, goes to great lengths to seek out thoughts and opinions that differ from his with the total objective of consistently making the most fact-based decisions possible. In Annie Duke's *Thinking in Bets*, the most successful woman's poker player describes how most people are biased toward supporting their own viewpoints. She makes a compelling case that the smarter we are, the more likely we are to be blinded to this bias.

If we are solely committed to proving our existing viewpoint is right, we are prevented from seeing alternatives, recognizing opportunities, and making creative, innovative decisions.

You Never Know Unless You Ask

The simple "you never know unless you ask" guideline that helped me generate a strong recurring revenue base applies to all aspects of life. Recently my sister told me that my fabulous niece, Julia, who was working three summer jobs, went to talk with her boss about a raise. After less than a minute, he said he was glad that she had come to see him; he absolutely agreed with what she'd told him about her work issues and hadn't been aware of the situation. He also thanked her for asking and yes, she got a significant raise.

When you want something, ask for it, especially if you have earned or deserve it. This is difficult for a lot of people. I'm not sure why, but I know it often relates to our childhood, when we were endlessly told "no" for all different reasons. As children most of us didn't accept "no" very easily. We asked and asked. If that didn't work, we changed our appeal and tried again. Even if we got rejected repeatedly, before long we were back at it.

What happens to us that we become afraid to ask for what we want? I'm not saying that you will always be thanked, as my niece was, for asking – or that you will get what you ask for. But you will get more of what you want if you ask. Your spouse, significant other, friends, and coworkers aren't mind readers. What would have happened if I had listened to Gary and hadn't tried to license our spreadsheets?

Ironically, even though I am almost always open to any suggestion, there are times when my first reaction is an instant no. In those situations I have either been too cautious, stubborn, or concerned about cost. Even though I don't always express this, I'm appreciative when someone pushes or promotes their idea despite my initial skepticism.

If you have a good idea or suggestion, don't just take no for an answer. Try to find out why the person says no. The most difficult, but critical, thing to do is to not take the rejection personally. Learn from the situation and be better prepared next time you talk with the person or face a similar situation.

Life Lessons from Mr. Lucky

Believe in yourself.

Be open to all ideas.

Look at things from multiple perspectives.

Don't let naysayers talk you out of a viable idea.

Quantify the impact of your proposals; be specific.

Be prepared and fact-based.

Keep it simple.

Prioritize the "most important stuff" and see that it gets done.

Don't take no personally. Identify the decision-maker's concerns; then revise and resubmit.

CHAPTER 9
Another Lucky Night

One lucky night early in the spring of 1999, I turned on my TV to watch the Braves game. The message I saw on the screen from DirecTV indicated that something was blocking the signal. Being a determined individual, I grabbed a ladder and, for the first time in my life, climbed onto the roof. Sure enough, a branch was blocking the satellite dish. I used a pair of scissors to trim the branch back a little.

Climbing up the ladder and walking around on the roof were easy, so I assumed going down would be just as simple. I had put the ladder on a tilt, thinking that this would make it easier to climb. Turns out that this is the exact opposite of what I should have done. As a result, on the way down I flew through the air face first – or should I say fell straight down onto the cement pool deck.

My right arm and the area just above my lip hit the ground at the same time. I lay there barely moving, as I was in shock, bleeding, and in pain. Finally I screamed out for my daughter, since my wife was at a concert in Chastain Park. Mel quickly arrived and seeing how badly I was hurt did what any four-and-a-half-year-old would do: She asked if I wanted a Band-Aid because of course they make pain go away!

Surprisingly, when I asked her to get the phone and call her friend Hannah's house, she knew the number. Luckily Hannah's dad, Eric, was at his home three houses away with his two precious daughters, because his wife was at the concert with Dawn. They quickly came over, and Eric drove us all to the hospital. Fortunately, Mr. Lucky only had a broken arm and needed two stitches to sew up the area above his lip.

If you are wondering WTF I was thinking climbing on the roof with a pair of scissors, I totally agree with you. Even now I am laughing at what a fool I was.

In my defense, I'm a get-stuff-done-now guy, which works most of the time. Recently, however, I started recognizing that we are all wired differently. I used to be bothered when I would get up from watching TV to get some water or a snack and my wife or daughter would ask me to get them something too. Not a big deal, right? But I used to think, *Why don't you get up and get it yourself? Sitting isn't good for you, and taking a few more steps is good as well.* Now I usually think, *Sure, my pleasure. You just relax.*

I am so lucky to have these women in my life. Even that fall from the roof turned out to be lucky. How is breaking your arm a lucky thing? Had I landed just a little differently or not partially broken the fall with my arm, the doctor said my nose would have gone straight into my brain and I could have been severely paralyzed.

Life is all about perspective. A "woe is me" attitude wears you down and isn't fun to be around. Stuff happens all the time; little stuff, big stuff. Pick yourself up. Look at the bright side. See the humor in your flaws; not one of us is perfect. This isn't easy, but once you start viewing your situation and the world with a glass-half-full attitude, you will be happier. I guarantee it. Nothing can stop you except yourself.

Life Lessons from Mr. Lucky

Band-Aids don't fix everything.

Don't take yourself so seriously.

Find the good, especially when things seem bad.

CHAPTER 10
Free Money

My biggest life lesson related to money involved watching my dad during the stock market's "free money" days in the late 1990s. My dad, along with lots of other folks, was making money hand over fist. The NASDAQ composite index rose 85.6 percent in 1999. Qualcomm, the best performing stock of the year, rose 2,619 percent; and there were twelve other stocks that rose by over 1,000 percent and seven more that went up by over 900 percent. The IPO market was crazy. As an example, the FreeMarkets IPO was planned to come to market at between $14 and $16 but it opened at $48 a share and ended the day at $290. People were making a killing; there was free money everywhere.

At this point in our lives, my dad and I spoke frequently, usually daily but at least once a week. We exchanged thoughts and ideas, and I greatly appreciated being able to talk with him about everything. We generally agreed about most things, but the stock market was one area where we disagreed – and not just a little. Since he was a broker, keeping our investments with him was logical if for nothing else than lower fees.

My sixty-year-old dad would kid me about being such a conservative investor. If not wanting to invest in companies with no earnings and sometimes barely any revenue is your definition of being conservative, then yes, I was, and still am, very conservative.

As I watched my dad rake in the money in the late '90s and early 2000, I would constantly ask him questions like, "How much is enough?" "What more are you going to do with the next million?" And of course, "Aren't you worried about the market correcting?" "Why don't you pull a chunk out just in case?" His answers were always along the line of, "It's easy money; why are you such a worrier?"

In case you don't remember what happened, the NASDAQ market peaked on March 10, 2000, and it fell by 78 percent over the following thirty months. I am fairly certain that my dad lost close to 90 percent of his investments during that time. Holy smokes, how could he be so stupid? I still can't believe that someone with years of experience in the business could make such a rookie mistake. Yet similar things happen all the time. I'm not sure if it's due to greed, fear of missing out, naïveté, or optimism bias – or some combination of all of these.

Leading up to the great recession, people did virtually the same thing in the housing market. Flippers made a killing until the market tanked and they lost most, or all, of their money. I'm not smart enough to figure out crypto-currencies but a lot of people have already been hurt chasing the easy money. Just the other day I was told how lucrative the high-end sneaker market can be. Wow!

I have yet to hear of any prudent ways to get rich quick. If you feel compelled to try, limit your highly speculative investments to no more than five percent of your net worth.

Losing it All

Watching my dad lose most of his money and later struggling to accept and juggle his financial situation has definitely impacted my beliefs about money;

how Dawn and I invest our money; and how I treat money. My friend Joyce Golinsky said it best years later when I sold my business, US Banking Alliance: "It's like you won the lottery except it's so much better because you earned it!" I completely agree and believe that this affects my overall thought process about money. I know how hard we worked to get it, and I'm protective of it since we are retired and may never earn any more. In the couple of one-off investments we have made, I've always wanted to see who else has put in their money and how much have they risked.

Seeing my dad lose what most people would consider a fortune probably helps explain why I often worry about money even though we have enough. Money is highly personal and not something people usually talk about; however, given its importance I thought I would share some of my thoughts and beliefs throughout the book. So much of how we deal with different aspects of our life typically comes from watching and listening to our parents. When it came to managing or spending money, my parents had two totally different philosophies.

Even in the early days when Mom and Dad were still married to one another, my dad was the risk-taker. Since he was a stockbroker, he constantly saw "big opportunities" to make more. As Mom told me, unfortunately, these opportunities often created significant financial strain, since they had no savings to fall back on when the stock or commodity markets didn't move the way they were "supposed to."

This issue became real for me when it came time to go to college. I was fortunate in that my parents paid for me to go to college and I graduated with no debt. That said, the reality was that the majority of the cost was covered by my mother, which in truth probably means that my stepfather, Bob, paid for it. He was always extremely generous with us all, especially my mother, which greatly benefited my sister and me.

I deeply appreciate this assistance, although for a long time I resented that the support did not come from my father. Even though her remarks were fair and accurate, I did not like hearing my mother say that my dad was not contributing his share.

I remember on one college break, my dad came to pick me up in his dream car, a Rolls-Royce. The car was just as gaudy and ostentatious as you can imagine, although it wasn't nearly as extravagant as it probably sounds because it was old – but not in a valuable way. Why in the world did he buy that car at the same time he was telling me and my mom he didn't have the money for his share of my college expenses?

My mom, as you can probably guess, was the fiscally conservative, responsible parent. She was a terrific schoolteacher, is a very intelligent person who understands financial markets and investing, and is a Silver Life Master bridge player. When I was growing up, Mom always stressed education, honesty, sharing, and being responsible. I love my mother, appreciate her teaching, and am delighted that she is still an important part of my life. Looking back, one thing my sister and I laugh about is that when I was in high school, she left me home to take care of my sister when she traveled. I'm not complaining but I'm not sure how responsible that was!

Given that many of my early lessons about money were from family, I am grateful that I had my mother's example to offset my father's.

Life Lessons from Mr. Lucky

Understand the risks you're taking.

Don't risk more than you can afford.

CHAPTER 11

Start of US Banking Alliance

I would love to tell you that I had a detailed business plan and a lifelong dream to build a loan-pricing solution from nothing to the best in the market and sell the business six years later. The actual story is much more modest, although I did actually achieve this result. In mid-2000, I came to an agreement with USBA to purchase my tiny division of four people through an earn-out.

The deal basically gave me everything I had helped create, including all the marketing materials, prospect information, and about fifteen licensing contracts for the Excel spreadsheets. This also gave me the exclusive right to the name US Banking Alliance. I originally wasn't sure if this was a positive or a negative, since the company had a somewhat checkered past and was selling or closing all of the other divisions.

The earn-out structure meant that the majority of the first year's profits went to the seller, but I had little risk as I could just walk away from the agreement any time during the year if things didn't go well. Also, once they received a predetermined amount of the profits, I would own 100 percent of the company. This ended up taking nine months.

I had considered leaving USBA and starting a one-person consulting company a couple of times over the previous three or four years. Even though management primarily left me alone, meaning I felt no urgency to leave, USBA wasn't a great place to work. In fact, I'm almost certain that the company lost money each year of its existence.

On the flip side, I enjoyed my working relationship with the owner's son, Steve Cotton, and folks like Curry Pelot and Jefferson Harralson, who worked in his group. I respected Steve's work ethic and integrity. He earned everything that he accomplished and worked twice as hard as most people in the company, never once taking advantage of, or benefiting from, nepotism.

At that point, I was reasonably confident that based on my reputation in the industry, I could earn at least as much as I was making as a consultant. Even though Dawn encouraged me to go out on my own, ultimately I chose the security of a paycheck.

The reality of my situation was pretty clear in 2000, with the company selling or closing divisions. I knew that if I could strike a reasonable deal with the company, I wouldn't have to start from scratch. The seller knew that if they asked for too much, I would leave the company, start my own, and they would get nothing. I had been an outstanding employee and had had a good yet limited relationship with the owner, Jim Cotton, for the previous thirteen years. I hired an attorney to help me with the legal aspect of the transaction, and thankfully things went smoothly.

Business Partners

Joel Rosenberg worked for me at USBA and did an excellent job, so I definitely wanted him to be part of my new company. Joel was very excited about the prospect and wanted to be a partner in the business. I don't recall the specifics of our conversations, but at one point he even offered to contribute capital to the business as part of becoming a minority partner. I didn't pursue this option.

I consider myself fortunate that Joel came on board only as an employee. Joel contributed significantly to the success of the organization, and I don't believe we would have been nearly as successful without him. He knew banking, particularly asset/liability management, as well as anyone. His math skills were exceptional, and he played a large role in enhancing the value of our Excel spreadsheets.

When we hired Carl Ryden to rescue our software development effort, Joel worked well with Carl and helped facilitate the transition from the Excel spreadsheets to real software. Joel was also a very good consultant, totally focused on delivering quality service and maintaining a strong, ongoing relationship with our clients.

As valuable as Joel was, I don't think the business would have been as successful if we had formed a partnership. I don't have a lot of empirical research to back up this statement, but I believe most relationships, business and personal, don't last. As a result, if you have the resources to start a business on your own, I suggest taking this route.

Keys to Success

The key factors that helped US Banking Alliance become successful were threefold: a fantastic product; a dedicated staff focused on delivering excellent service; and a belief that what we were offering was the best and most important solution in the industry.

The most significant thing I can say is that each aspect of the business depended on the other, and that the focus on improvement and the striving for excellence was nonstop. I love sports and think business is a lot like sports. A championship team is usually well-balanced, with a couple of strengths and no glaring deficiencies. It's always fun to watch a superstar, but without teamwork and a good supporting cast they usually won't go all the way. A great coach is essential, but they too need great players to be successful.

Our solution consisted of consulting (loan and deposit strategies); Excel spreadsheets (real software came later); training on their use; a written report that documented the strategies; and unlimited implementation assistance. We believed there wasn't a bank in the country that wouldn't benefit from our solution and we guaranteed a return of at least twice our fee, usually delivering much more.

Sometimes a bank would only want the spreadsheets or only the strategies and not the whole solution. We would tell them that we could give them our software and they wouldn't get any benefit. Or we could give them our consulting report and they wouldn't get any benefit. We totally believed in our approach and weren't willing to take their money unless they purchased the whole solution.

Our software was quick and easy to use and our strategies were straight-forward and easy to implement. In fact, we could go to a bank for two and a half days and change their entire approach to pricing, which was the most impactful aspect of their business. Believe it or not, most banks don't know the profitability of the loans that they are putting on their books. This has always been truly shocking to me and the key to my business. The most critical thing that a bank does is lend money, and they do it all day long without knowing the profitability!

Even though implementing our solution was quick and easy, we knew that without going through the entire process they would not be successful. They needed us to challenge their traditional, long-held beliefs around loan and deposit pricing, specifically the emotional and behavioral issues associated with their long-term, unprofitable customers. This had to be fully addressed so that when the bankers sat across the desk from their clients and prospects, they wouldn't revert to their previous, habitual ways.

Prove It to Me

Bankers are skeptical people by nature, especially the credit people. Loan pricing software has been around forever and *never* once had I heard a bank say that they liked the system they were using.

In 1998, when Gary told me he was going to create some loan pricing spreadsheets for our clients, I was initially against the idea. I absolutely believed that the world had enough loan pricing software that was either hated or sitting on a shelf not being used. We talked through the issue and agreed that the key was to create something that was quick and easy to use, with a focus on enhancing the relationship between the borrower and the bank. Gary created something valuable that Joel Rosenberg and others would help take to the next level.

Given the dislike for loan pricing models, we typically started each strategy session at the bank with a group of lenders who had their arms crossed and a "prove it to me" expression on their faces. I believed it was crucial to win over the lenders and management team in the first sixty minutes, and our approach was geared toward ensuring this. When we left the bank, they needed to be up and running, using our software, and ready to implement the strategies.

The next thirty days were also crucial, as the more momentum we created, the greater the likelihood that the client would be successful in the long run. We were extremely proud that 97 percent of our clients renewed their licensing agreements each year. This was essential for building our recurring revenue stream, and we were able to confidently state this to our prospects, who were concerned that what we offered was too good to be true. Our guarantee to increase their earnings by at least two times our fee was usually viewed skeptically, even though clients typically achieved five or ten times the fee.

You would think the guarantee would be very helpful, and in many ways it was, but we also spent a fair amount of time explaining what we meant and that it wasn't a trick or a gimmick. After a couple of years, we changed our guarantee to be a simple satisfaction guarantee. We wrote the guarantee to be one line of our contract, totally biased toward the client in an effort to minimize their apprehension. This helped but still didn't completely eliminate their doubt.

We provided unlimited implementation assistance for similar reasons; I wanted the most satisfied clients possible, as they were likely to provide referrals and strong references. Jeffrey Gitomer, author of many helpful sales books and a blogger whom I highly recommend, stated that satisfied clients were not the goal; you want raving fans, and anything less leaves you vulnerable to the competition and pricing issues.

Great Opportunities

Everybody's job, especially the people in sales, is easier and more fun when you have happy clients. In addition to references and referrals, our clients helped by recommending us to speak at industry conferences. Two opportunities were particularly significant for our company. The first occurred when Ken Heiser, from FNB Hudson, recommended that I present at the American Bankers Association's National Conference for Community Bankers in Palm Beach, CA.

I remember this presentation not only because it was my biggest audience, but also because my luggage didn't arrive. I was especially nervous that day and started by making a joke about being inappropriately dressed. Thankfully the audience laughter loosened me up and gave me confidence. When I finished, several people asked for my business card or gave me theirs and requested that I call them to discuss our services.

Even though I never became a great speaker, I was successful because I was extremely knowledgeable about the subject matter and spoke with the conviction of a person who believed we could help every single bank. As a result, most of our growth came from my speaking engagements. I tailored presentations around the effective use of loan pricing software. I always walked a fine line of not selling (a total no-no for a speaker) while demonstrating principles and concepts showing our model. I would clearly state that I was using our software and jokingly say that I definitely wasn't going to use someone else's.

My presentations would typically focus on the key factors that made banks successful or caused them to be ineffective in their implementation of pricing software. My goal was for prospective clients to see how powerful and easy it was to use good loan pricing software. Invariably one or two people would criticize me in the speaker evaluations for selling, but I truly believed that I provided more value than any of the other more polished and eloquent speakers.

The most significant piece of advice I can give about public speaking is to join a group like Toastmasters to become more comfortable. Also recognize that the objective isn't to make an excellent presentation; it's to grow your business. Obviously if you want to be asked to speak in the future, you need to make a good speech. Additionally, make sure the topic is something closely aligned with your product or service so that you actually benefit from all the time and energy involved.

I almost always started my presentations with a quick, five-question quiz that challenged the audience to carefully assess their loan pricing process. It was rare that anybody except our clients were able to answer three or more of these simple questions about their own process. This always got the audience's attention, and then I showed them how easy and impactful it was to address the issue. I had a similar philosophy and approach to writing articles for industry publications.

The second significant speaking opportunity occurred about eighteen months later, with the Bank CEO Network. This was a group of roughly 180 bankers (two or three were my clients) that met twice a year. I was asked to facilitate three-hour sessions for twelve to twenty bankers, once or twice a day over a two-week period. This was a major success, as three years later about eighty of these banks were our clients. In general, bankers talk among themselves and this group formed especially close relationships, so I can say with certainty that the reason for our success was simple. We delivered everything we said we would and more, including overwhelming value, for each bank.

I used the word *value* because of its importance to pricing. We were the most expensive solution provider by a significant amount. I was never bashful about price. In fact, I took pride in our high fee and felt we earned our money by always delivering for our clients. I would rarely even negotiate price. When I did, I would make a big deal about how important they were to us because they were our first client in a given market, or some other justifiable reason, and then I would only offer the smallest discount.

We didn't win every deal but we almost never lost to a competitor. More times than not, if a bank didn't hire us it was because they decided to do nothing. Some people might not view this as losing, but I did. This meant that we had not convinced them that our approach was worth the cost and effort to make a change.

Life Lessons from Mr. Lucky

Finding a great business partner is extremely difficult.

A satisfied client is not enough.

Speaking at industry conferences can be great but be careful how you define a great presentation.

Reduce or eliminate your prospect's risk.

Earn the right to charge a high fee.

Deliver tremendous value relative to your cost.

CHAPTER 12
Joy in Dying

When Dawn and I got married on August 26, 1989, my wacky but sweet mother-in-law, Russell Wishnie, lived in Oakland, California, approximately 2,460 miles away from our home in Atlanta. What could be more perfect? Then less than two months later, on October 17th, thirty-one minutes before game three of the World Series between her Oakland A's and the San Francisco Giants, an earthquake struck. This scared Russell and a couple of months later she decided to move closer to her family: 2,458 miles closer, to be exact.

We had some fun times together, including taking Mel to an Olympic baseball game when she was just eighteen months old, and some interesting times, such as when Atlanta had an ice storm and we lost power. Dawn, Mel, our two dogs, and I spent a couple of nights with Russell and her dog in her tiny one-bedroom apartment.

My earliest memory of Russell dates from three days after Dawn and I got engaged. We flew from our ski trip in Utah, where I proposed on the top of Snowbird Mountain, to Oakland for Russell's fiftieth birthday party. I wasn't expecting a crazy fun party with people dressed in drag.

Other than my frustration with her being a little nutty and more like a daughter than a mother to Dawn, Russell and I had a good relationship. I'm glad my daughter was able to spend a few years with her grandmama before she died. Looking back, I wish I had known her during a period of my life when I wasn't so focused on work so I could have been more supportive. Today I'm much more empathetic to other people's challenges, although I still struggle with those who don't take control of their own lives, and I don't think Russell did.

On March 8, 2000, Dawn called me when I was on the road to inform me that her sixty-one-year-old mother had received a completely unexpected diagnosis: stage four adrenal cancer. She was immediately placed in hospice where, believe it or not, she enjoyed three of the happiest weeks of her life before she peacefully passed on March 30.

During one of the last conversations Dawn had with her mother, Russell expressed total amazement that friend after friend came from all over the world to tell her how much she had meant to them and how much they loved her. She felt overwhelmed by the gifts they had given her. Dawn said, "Mom, it's been that way your whole life. We just had a sixtieth birthday party for you last year. People came from everywhere. Everyone loves you and has always told you how much you mean to them." Her mom told her that she finally felt like she deserved it.

Last year, Dawn sadly recalled her mother's deathbed words and told me, "I don't want to live like that." She continued, "I want to be able to give *and* receive love." Then she laughed a little and said, "I know it's not something I'm great at, but I'm working on it." We talked about how most people, including us, often don't even know how to accept a compliment. Dawn mentioned that years ago she noticed that her cousin Beth was good at simply saying "Thank you" when she receives a compliment. Dawn tries to graciously receive compliments but finds it still can be difficult.

I'm so glad that Dawn's mother had such a special end-of-life experience and finally got the message that so many of us, including me, have such a difficult time receiving and remembering. We all have many people who love and appreciate us, and we need to cut ourselves some slack and recognize that we are worthy of the love.

Life Lessons from Mr. Lucky

Learn to accept compliments.

Cut yourself some slack.

Remember you are worthy of love.

CHAPTER 13
Selling Very Differently

nother key member of the US Banking Alliance team was our salesman, John Whetstone. He was so disciplined that he worked out of his house because he didn't want to waste time in Atlanta's crazy traffic or with the typical office interruptions. Most workdays John walked into his home office at 8:00 and put on his headset. He typically called bankers until 6:00 with a short break for lunch if he had time. His calls were organized by time zone and ranked by importance so that he made the most of each day.

When I met John in 1999, we worked in two separate groups at USBA. Early in his career John was the CFO at a bank, so he understood the importance of our solution and believed that all banks needed it. John thought our offering was so good that he literally begged me to let him sell it. We originally came to an agreement for him to work for my group half a day, with the other half-day spent selling a compliance product.

A short time later, when I started my company, John was so confident that he would be successful, he offered to join me for $12,000 a year plus a generous commission structure. I am not sure how much money he made the first year, but John quickly became the highest-paid employee, exceeding the top end of his revised commission plan each year.

A couple of years later I hired two more salespeople. I have looked back to try to determine why John was so successful and they weren't. I think there were two big differences. First, John had worked in the business and knew and understood why every bank needed our solution. Second, neither of the other salespeople utilized me in the sales process nearly as much as John did.

The way our sales process worked was straightforward. The salespeople would follow up on leads from our speaking engagements. Their goal was to schedule a webcast with the bank. After the webcast, which I primarily led, they would try to include me in any call that was likely to be meaningful until a deal was closed. I made numerous calls with John every day and very few with the other sales associates. The objective of the calls was always twofold. We needed to understand all of the concerns of the key decision-makers and address them. Once this was accomplished, we wanted them to call our references.

A subtle point when addressing a prospect's concerns is to truly understand what they are asking and what they may not be asking or saying. A person who is completely knowledgeable about the solution will be aware of this and able to read and react to the situation appropriately. I think this is one of the most difficult things to teach a salesperson and I don't think either of our other two sales associates appreciated these subtleties.

When I think further about what made us successful selling our solution, I believe that our discipline and determination were significant, but there was one factor that was critical. I challenged the beliefs of the bank's executive management team, whether I was speaking at a conference, writing an article, or making a sales presentation. I was not afraid to disagree with them during a sales presentation or a follow-up call. In fact, I didn't view this as a problem; I actually thought this created the big opportunity.

Our solution required banks to think totally differently about loan pricing, something they had been doing for years. They either thought they were doing it well or that they didn't have control over pricing because of the competition. Neither of these views was accurate. An excellent book, *The Challenger Sale* by Matthew Dixon and Brent Adamson, written after I sold the business, focuses on the importance of taking control of a conversation when you want to teach someone what they should know but they don't.

We had to teach banks a whole new way of thinking about pricing and customer relationships. This is very different than traditional relationship selling, where the salesperson works with the prospect to give them what they already know they need or want. Relationship selling works well for selling real estate or automobiles but, as the authors determined in their research, it doesn't work for selling a complex solution.

Neither John nor I were classically trained salespeople. We examined our sales process informally just about every week and formally each month, challenging each other about what we thought was working and not, looking at the little words or phrases that seemed to resonate. We didn't use scripts or rely on rules, because they don't work well for a complex sale.

We relied on our knowledge of banking, especially loan pricing. There was nothing that anyone could ask me or tell me that would throw me off. I would try to relate their questions and issues to a real live situation at their bank or a similar bank. This level of knowledge is difficult to find in a traditional salesperson and it would be virtually impossible to train a salesperson to close this type of sale.

Don't Be Afraid to Be Different

While rules and scripts don't work, having a good sales process – knowing step by step what is needed to get prospects from the start of the sales pipeline all the way to the close – is essential. I will talk about a few of the things I learned in this area; many of them the hard way.

We would not make a presentation unless the CEO was at the meeting. After many failed attempts at "making the presentation anyway," we learned that the CEO would be scared off if they heard our price before fully understanding the opportunity. As a result, we even canceled webcasts right as they were about to start if the CEO had a last-minute conflict. This was as awkward as it sounds. But remember the goal wasn't to make a great presentation; it was to create another raving client.

We also learned not to skip any steps in the sales process. As exciting as it was when the prospect said they were going to hire us before they had talked to our references or had a discussion between their IT people and ours, this always ended up delaying the sale, not speeding it up.

Another factor that helped us considerably was that we had one solution and we stayed focused entirely on enhancing it. In the first eighteen months of our business, I was asked to help a prospect with their investment portfolio. I sized up the opportunity and decided that even though the fee would have been nice, we should pass. I felt qualified to deliver what they needed but didn't believe that this would enhance our business, and it would distract me from what really needed to be done.

Identifying and monitoring the key factors to your long-term success is essential to growing your business. While I was definitely happy whenever we made a sale, I was equally focused on four other factors: how many speaking opportunities were scheduled; the number of upcoming webcasts; how many were done in the last month; and how well each engagement went. I knew that we needed to speak at the conferences to gather our prospects; then make a presentation (webcast); and finally close the deal. Of course, the most essential step of all was to deliver far in excess of what we promised.

Very Different

One aspect of our sales process was completely different from the typical consulting or software company. Over 99 percent of the business I generated with USBA and US Banking Alliance occurred without ever going to the prospect's office. In most cases we never even met anyone from the bank in person prior to being hired, although they may have seen me speak at a conference. Typically, the bank's senior management team was in a conference room with a speakerphone and handouts (prior to a webcast being an option). I would walk them through a presentation that was both technical and theoretical.

I'm not saying that this was an easy way to hold a sales meeting. The biggest drawback was that you couldn't read and react to people's body language. Additionally, things didn't always go as smoothly as I would have liked because of an echo or a slight delay, so people would end up talking over one another. One advantage of a conference call was that it forced you to check in many times during the presentation to draw out questions and probe for areas of disagreement.

Things got a little easier when I was able to upgrade to a webcast for our sales presentations. At USBA, only one other department – out of more than a dozen – sold their product or services this way. Coincidentally, we were also the only two departments that didn't lose money.

At US Banking Alliance thirty percent of the banks that did a webcast with us became clients, so I think it's fair to say we were effective. This approach had several added benefits, including that we proved to our prospects upfront that we would usually be able to help them after the onsite engagement without having to go to their office. This saved the clients money and also helped reduce the travel burden on our sales and consulting teams.

Our approach proved that you didn't have to do the standard sales "press the flesh" bull that most say is necessary. I challenge anyone reading this who thinks it doesn't apply to their situation; we weren't making quick or easy sales. The cost of our service was large enough that board of directors' approval was needed most of the time.

Twenty years later technology has improved, and getting on a plane, or multiple planes, and then driving to a prospect's office has gotten more difficult. Think about how much more productive your salespeople would be if they didn't have to travel, and how much it would lower your expenses.

I want to be clear: I'm not saying that there is never a need for onsite sales meetings. I am saying that perhaps 10 or 20 or even 50 percent of these meetings could take place via webcast.

I know the approach I have just described is counter to so many companies that I want to defend this position further. The sales process at FNN/USBA and many companies had built-in biases that resulted in higher costs for the consulting firm, which inevitably increased the cost to the client or reduced profitability. I often saw situations in which a prospect expressed what seemed like some interest, along the lines of "Next time you're in the area stop by." The salesperson would often magically be in the area the next week.

The high cost for such hastily scheduled sales trips is usually quickly overlooked because relative to the revenue that can be booked from a big deal, the costs don't seem so high. Also, salespeople usually get paid to win deals, not to save money. In fact, they lose their job for not making sales – not for making too many trips. Are these trips truly needed? Are they actually increasing the likelihood of eventually closing the deal?

How many of your sales meetings are scheduled at the last minute? In addition to the higher travel costs, the likelihood of the prospect getting all the right people into a last-minute meeting isn't good, thereby compromising the potential value of a meeting. These hastily scheduled meetings also have a higher propensity to get canceled at the last minute, which is another indication that the meeting wasn't properly vetted to ensure value.

When the cost of a sales meeting is considered, most people don't even begin to account for what else the salesperson could have done in the day of travel time that was needed to meet for one or two hours.

I don't mean to minimize the value of relationships in sales or business. As I have mentioned, US Banking Alliance relied heavily on our clients to help grow our business, both through referrals and references. Our primary objective during sales presentations was to convince prospects that they had a meaningful opportunity to improve the most important aspect of their business. Since prospects almost always downplay what salespeople tell them, another goal was to get them to call our existing clients. We wanted the prospects to hear directly from clients how powerful our impact was on their bank.

Life Lessons from Mr. Lucky

Becoming a great salesperson is difficult.

Finding great salespeople is a challenge.

Having discipline and determination is half the battle – but only half.

Relationship selling is not always appropriate. Read *The Challenger Sale*.

Identify every step in the sales process.

Establish a great sales process and monitor its success.

Don't make presentations unless the key decision-makers are involved.

Evaluate how technology can reduce your sales cost and travel.

Maximize the impact of clients as references.

Challenge the status quo often.

CHAPTER 14

Speak Up, John

On many occasions I brusquely asked my salesman, John, to speak up. I assumed that if I couldn't hear him, our prospects couldn't either. In hindsight, I obviously wasn't as patient as I should have been with John. He had a strong work ethic but we were definitely wired differently. John was perfect for his role: consistent, steady, and disciplined. Most importantly, he didn't let my occasional moodiness stop us from having an excellent working relationship.

One lucky day I picked up my headset and put it on in a way that was basically backwards. Instead of having the ear cover over my left ear, it was over my right ear. All of a sudden I could not only hear John much better, but it was loud. When I realized what had happened, I tried the handheld phone with each ear and found that the hearing in my left ear was far less than my right ear.

I quickly made an appointment with an ear specialist, Dr. Terrence Murphy. He determined that my hearing was off by about forty decibels in the left ear, and he found a skin growth, cholesteatoma, that needed to be removed. He scheduled my surgery for August 27th, the day after our wedding anniversary. The night before surgery Dawn and I went out to celebrate at our favorite Italian restaurant in Atlanta, La Grotta.

I can picture the table where we were sitting and clearly recall our conversation. This was my first operation and they had warned me of all the risks associated with the surgery. None of them were the least bit appealing, especially being paralyzed. Even though the odds of anything negative occurring were slim, I remember being extremely nervous.

That night we talked about dying. Dawn actually enjoys talking about death. Not in a morbid way; it's just that she recognizes that it is a part of life. For me this was definitely not a comfortable discussion, particularly on our anniversary. Even now I almost never think about dying. I'll be sixty years old in a few months and I'm enjoying life. I'm sure that most young people think that sixty is old.

Let me tell you that age is just a number. I'm in excellent health, and my daughter is always saying that I have a lot more fun than she does. I'm going to concerts, sporting events, and taking amazing trips that involve a high level of physical activity. When I set my alarm it's because I want to get up for something, not because I have to. Most important, I now have time to do things that will make a difference in the world.

I obviously didn't die during my surgery, although what had been scheduled for two to three hours took over five hours. Mr. Lucky dodged another bullet as the skin growth, which was much larger than anticipated, was right up against the thin membrane wall to the brain. Dawn remembers Dr. Murphy saying he actually saw my brain.

Life Lessons from Mr. Lucky

Be grateful for every day – be grateful every day – be grateful.

CHAPTER 15

US Banking Alliance: Your People Matter

Work Hard and Figure Things Out

I am forever grateful for people like Laurie Smith, who started out as my administrative assistant. Laurie graduated cum laude with a marketing degree from the University of Dayton. She worked with me from day one at US Banking Alliance, and I don't know how the company would have done without her. She stepped in and took on whatever role needed to be filled and figured things out fearlessly. In the end I think she was our personnel manager, office manager, accounting and payroll clerk, and my executive assistant. I don't mean that she held all those jobs during her time with the company; I mean that her job consisted of doing them all at once!

Laurie had a very good work ethic and would go into the office on Saturday every few weeks to catch up. I never once had to ask her to do this, but I greatly appreciated walking into the office on Sunday or Monday morning and seeing that her desk was back to normal. Laurie's calm demeanor helped balance me out, as I worked intensely all day long on multiple things. Laurie was also my eyes and ears when I was on the road.

The most valuable aspect of our relationship was that I trusted Laurie, even with the money! Laurie handled all the bills and the majority of our banking, including being a signer on the corporate account. I always had simple spreadsheets on which I kept track of sales and cash flow, and I scrutinized our monthly financials. Still, we didn't have a board of directors or anyone else looking at the numbers except our accountants. They did a relatively quick review quarterly and prepared my taxes annually.

I remember calling my accountant twice and telling him that I totally trusted Laurie, but when he reviewed our books to bear in mind that she probably had more access to our money than was prudent. Thankfully, he always called with good news and took away that one percent of doubt I had. My other concern about Laurie was completely selfish and I am almost ashamed to admit it. I worried that she would get pregnant and either take maternity leave or become a stay-at-home mom.

This concern ties in to one of the challenging early periods of the company, when Laurie went on vacation. At that point things were still simple from an administrative standpoint. However, we almost always had a couple of proposals and a client report that needed to be finished. I mistakenly thought this could be handled by my wife, who had been successful in the corporate world before taking the far more challenging job of stay-at-home mom.

Much to my surprise this did not go well, and I learned that family and business are not a good combination. I still wonder if this was one of those situations in which your spouse asks you do to something and you decide not to do it well, hoping that you won't be asked again! That said, my amazing wife supported me in every other way.

Hiring Your Best Friend – Oh No

Everyone has probably heard the advice not to lend money or go into business with family and friends. The lure to do both is strong, and there are obviously many situations where everything works out well. My experience ignoring both of these time-tested warnings did not. I will share these stories in the hope that some of you can avoid the tremendous pain that can come from disregarding such longstanding wisdom. Making mistakes is a natural, and necessary, part of our journey. But the cost associated with some is far greater than with others, and for me these errors were the most painful.

I first mentioned Courtney Dufries when I talked about getting a job at the Federal Reserve Bank of Atlanta (the Fed) in 1984. We quickly became friends and three years later, when I left, we were very good friends. Over the next ten-plus years he was like family to me, and to this day my daughter often refers to him as Uncle Courtney.

About a year after I started my company, we talked about how awesome it would be to work together. Roughly a year later we got serious about it. Courtney was making a good living at the Fed, but nobody gets rich working there. That said, when you hit the milestones needed to retire, the pension is fantastic, so there was a considerable downside to him leaving. I drew up a short document that provided salary levels and an equity stake based on him meeting certain performance levels. The agreement was mostly subjective, and I had total control to determine whether he achieved the objectives, so what could possibly go wrong? After all, we were best friends!

Looking back I now see that we were doomed from the beginning. Almost by definition, the best relationships are between two people or organizations where things are equal. Up until this point, as best friends we each brought different things to the relationship, and at the end of the day we had the utmost respect for one another.

Courtney left his job at the Federal Reserve Bank after working there for twenty years and being extremely successful. He was recognized as an industry expert in Community Affairs and was knowledgeable about the banking industry. However, he had only a basic knowledge about loan and deposit pricing. The big problem was that his best friend, who was an expert in this area, was going to teach him and make him the best in the business.

You see where this is going. Courtney knew his old job cold, but he was no longer fresh out of college. It had been basically twenty years since he'd been told what to do and how to do it. Now he was being shown by me and Joel, our senior consultant, how to do every little thing, and doing things well wasn't good enough. Each client was integral to our success, so I wanted everything to be as close to perfect as possible.

Don Julio

Imagine finishing up a day on which you did a five-hour loan-pricing strategy session and a three-hour deposit-pricing session with the executive management team of a bank, and the client was overjoyed with the result. It's now six o'clock and you have a similar day scheduled for tomorrow. What would you want to do?

If you answered, "Sit in a room with Mitchell to dissect every word that I said so he could tell me any and every opportunity for improving my performance," you win the prize: a bottle of Don Julio 1942. (For those unfamiliar with Don Julio, this is a high-end tequila that is perfect for sipping. I urge you to do so without any ice.)

Back to the challenge: Our business was growing beautifully, and I honestly believed that every word not only mattered, but our long-term success depended on it. So in addition to the nightly critiques we would do one after each engagement, usually on the way to the airport. I didn't see any other way. Back in the office I was focused on selling, reviewing client reports, preparing for the next engagement, etc. Even if I had the time three days later, it would be difficult to remember everything exactly, so I figured we were better off doing it right away.

As you can probably imagine, this wasn't what Courtney had in mind when he came to work with me. I have to say Courtney became very good at his job, and I'm glad that he stuck it out until I sold the business. Regrettably, he wasn't the happiest guy in the office, and we had far too many sit-downs airing out our issues.

Difficult Decisions

The toughest issue relating to Courtney was the partnership agreement. While I believed that Courtney was a valuable employee, and clients liked and respected him, I did not believe that he had met the terms of our agreement. I thought that the best way to deal with the situation was to give him the financial benefits the partnership would have provided, such as the salary and ownership benefits in the event of a sale, without making him a partner.

This was disappointing and frustrating to both of us. Courtney had envisioned that we would be regularly strategizing on the business. While I valued his opinion most of the time, I definitely didn't want his opinion on everything. Basically, I didn't want anything slowing us down.

Looking back at my US Banking Alliance days, my biggest regret is the impact on my relationship with Courtney. By the time I sold the company we weren't doing much fun stuff together.

During the thirty days leading up to the sale of the business, the company that purchased us managed to totally alienate our entire management team. As such, Courtney was the first to leave shortly after the deal closed. I don't think the two of us spent any time together for the next couple of years.

When I visited Atlanta three or four years later, Courtney and I got together for lunch and caught up on each other's families and lives. A couple of years later we went to the ten-year anniversary of the Wanee Music Festival in Live Oak, Florida, featuring two nights of the Allman Brothers Band. We had a fantastic time, and although we still aren't getting together or talking regularly, I like to think it's because we live 511 miles apart. At this point I miss my buddy, and if I could have a do-over, I wouldn't have mixed business with friendship, as truly great friends are hard to come by.

Hire the Best

The last key piece to our team was Carl Ryden, who I usually describe as the smartest person I have ever met. Carl has an MBA, as well as a master's degrees in electrical engineering from MIT. His knowledge is exceeded by his humbleness, which is a rare quality, and his passion for excellence and his work ethic are second to none.

One Saturday morning Carl was talking about our company with his neighbor, who just happened to be Mr. Lucky's good friend Courtney. Carl thought our situation sounded very interesting, so Courtney introduced us to one another.

About a year earlier we had hired a programmer to convert our Excel spreadsheets into real software. While he could not have been a nicer guy, he was clearly not the right person to lead our software development process.

Carl initially came on board under a six-month contract and then full-time. He wrote the bulk of the initial code himself and methodically created a process for hiring a small software development team. He also quickly became part of the management team and greatly enhanced our overall hiring process.

My philosophy was to hire the most qualified people possible and pay them well. Even in the early days of my career, I tried to hire people who were smarter than me. I can't even begin to imagine hiring a less-qualified person in an attempt to make yourself look good. I wanted people like Carl, who would challenge me and refuse to take no for an answer when they were right.

As an example, we were using Act, a customer relationship management (CRM) system, when Salesforce, which is now the leading CRM system in the world, was just getting started. Carl saw how Salesforce could help us in almost every aspect of our business, so he recommended that we switch from Act to Salesforce. In addition to the cost, I was initially reluctant because I was concerned that during the conversion, we would lose some prospect notes. I also didn't want to slow down John, our salesperson, and have the entire company spend time learning to use a new system. Thankfully Carl was persistent in promoting his belief, and the new system became an integral part of how we operated.

Although I don't think others challenged me as frequently or with as much conviction, I think we succeeded in the hiring process. During the six years I owned the company, only one person resigned, and that occurred less than thirty days after he was hired.

Numerous studies show the cost to replace an employee is typically one to two times the person's annual salary. I believe that the cost is much more, especially for a small, growing company. Just think about the time it takes to interview and train new employees, as well as to clean up the mess from an underperformer. The more complex your product or solution, the higher the cost. If the problem is severe and you lose a client or two, the cost can be astronomical; certainly far more than one or two times the person's salary.

When You Make a Mistake, Fix It

One of the toughest parts of being the CEO is firing people. I'm not sure there is such a thing as being good at firing people, but I think any time I had to do it, I was fair. Since we were a small company and I was involved in every aspect of the business except software development, I had a good handle on what was going on in the company.

As I said, I'm a get-stuff-done guy with limited patience, so when I see an issue my first instinct is to do something about it. If it turned out that after a short period of time we were unable to coach a person up to par, I always believed the best solution for both the employee and the company was to go our separate ways. As strong as that belief was, I never enjoyed firing an employee and always felt sick to my stomach doing so.

I believe that once you have made a decision to let someone go, you should inform the person as quickly and as matter-of-factly as possible. Our policy was always to have a second person, usually Courtney, in my office when I had these difficult meetings. I was always overly generous with severance, as I believe that the company has a responsibility for everyone who is hired. They were working someplace else, earning a paycheck, when you each convinced one another that they were the right person for the job. After a brief discussion, Courtney would take the person back to his or her office, watch them pack their personal belongings, retrieve their office key, and escort them out.

My only regret in this regard was the time I had to let go of a salesperson who hadn't sold much. She was so insulted and hurt by the process of being escorted out. She said that our procedures made her feel like a criminal, as she would never have gone into our database and destroyed sales records, etc. I am 99 percent sure that no one we ever hired, especially this salesperson, would have done anything malicious on their way out. That said, as a business owner I was responsible for not only my family but for everyone else who worked for me, so I erred on the side of caution. Although I wouldn't do it differently, I still feel sorry that I made her feel that way.

Life Lessons from Mr. Lucky

Have a great work ethic.

Working with family and friends has a high level of risk.

Hire the most qualified and pay them well.

Listen to and respect the expertise of others.

The cost of a bad hire is very high.

Address your underperforming employees quickly and fairly.

CHAPTER 16

Oh My God, the House is on Fire!

Sunday night of Labor Day weekend in 2003, we had good friends over for dinner. We grilled ribs, played some board games, and drank some great wine. That night Dawn woke up at about 2:30 in the morning, as she usually does, to go to the bathroom. As she was getting up, she noticed a beautiful glow outside. Fortunately she took a quick look behind the window treatments to see the cause of this beauty.

Then she screamed. "Wake up, the house is on fire!"

I sat up immediately, as if I had been waiting all my life for this moment, and said, "You call 911 and I'll get Melanie!"

I grabbed nine-year-old Mel, our dog Rocky, wrapped myself in a towel, and raced out the door. Dawn threw on some clothes, grabbed our other dog Benny, along with her purse, and drove her car out of the driveway.

I jumped in her car, and we drove around the corner of our cul-de-sac, where we were able to see the back side of our house. Sure enough the house was on fire: big time. Moments later we saw two teenage boys from the neighborhood watching the fire as well. We explained that it was our house and asked them if I could borrow a pair of shorts and a tee shirt.

Even though the fire station was less than a mile away, the fire trucks took a long time to arrive. Finally, five fire trucks came screeching into the neighborhood with their sirens wailing. We drove our car halfway back to our house and parked where we had a good vantage point to see what was happening to our home. We lived in the Woodcliff subdivision off Johnson Ferry Road that had thirty-nine homes built between 1999 and 2001. Our house was at the end of the cul-de-sac farthest from the entrance.

Within minutes of the fire trucks arriving, over half of our neighbors were standing with us, watching our house burn down. I don't think I have experienced a more surreal feeling. Neighbors kept saying that I seemed so calm. I just kept repeating how lucky we were. The three of us had gotten out of the house with both of our dogs very easily. I was sure that somewhere, someone else had learned that they or a loved one had been diagnosed with cancer or had received some other devastating news. All we lost was stuff.

Thankfully, my wonderful wife with the tiny bladder had woken up just in time. At 2:30 in the morning, there hadn't been any fire or smoke inside the house. An hour later the entire roof of the house caved in. For some unknown reason, it took over thirty minutes until the firemen were actually doing something to stop the fire, even though there was a hydrant less than fifty yards from the front door.

I can't imagine how my daughter felt as she realized everything in the house was gone. Thank goodness I had unknowingly grabbed her blankie. I just kept saying to her, "It's only stuff; and imagine how we would feel if Rocky and Benny were stuck inside." At some point Dawn, Melanie, and I went into our neighbors' house, as we figured Melanie should try to get some sleep.

Did You Start that Fire?

A few minutes later I went back outside, and the night got even more intense as an extremely large, muscular man whose shirt read "Arson Police" strode up to me. He had some questions. What happened? I nervously told him about the night, which until 2:30 had seemed fun but rather unremarkable. Had there been any drinking? Yes, but nothing out of the ordinary, and we weren't drunk. Drugs? No. Did I turn off the gas grill, which was right next to my house? I told him I had. Was I sure? I answered, "Officer, I am as sure as I can be, except that my house just burned down so I'm *not quite one hundred percent* sure!"

Then he leaned in. Did I start the fire? No. Did I think my wife started the fire? No, I didn't. Did we arrange for someone to start the fire? No, sir. Are we having any financial problems? To put this in perspective, there were still a lot of people standing about ten feet away from us, watching the house burning down.

He continued his intense line of questioning. Are my wife and I having any problems I want to tell him about? No, we aren't having any problems. Next he asked to speak with my wife. I explained that she was inside with my daughter. Could he talk to her in the morning? No, I want to talk with her *now*. Yes, sir. I went and got her, and the two of them had a similar conversation.

As the sun was rising, the fire died. The chief told us he would meet us back here later in the morning so we could take a walk through the house. After a few hours of sleep, we went back outside to take a look. No, it hadn't been a dream, or should I say a nightmare. The inside of our beautiful stone and shingle house was totally burnt down. It was very eerie, in that if you took a quick look at the house from the front, it looked normal except that there was no roof. Once you walked in, it was total devastation. The framing that remained was entirely charred. We were able to walk up the stairs, but as you looked up you could see the sky.

One Lucky Catch

I remember looking into the area that was formerly my office and seeing a baseball lying among the rubble. I still wonder if it was the ball that Tom Glavine pitched to Brian Harper in Game 5 of the 1991 World Series. After it left Harper's bat it went way up in the air, right behind home plate. I thought it was going back about fifteen rows behind home plate, and we were sitting in row 13. Dawn thought differently, as she was slapping my leg to get up. At the last second, I jumped up on my seat, just about when the ball hit the hand of a guy two rows behind us. It popped up, and I was able to reach over the next row and catch it. What an exhilarating feeling as I held the ball and people clapped! Then everyone around us wanted to see it and touch it. No way was I going to let that ball out of my hands!

For some odd reason I didn't touch the ball or anything else in the house. I guess as calm as I'd been the night before, the lack of sleep and the shock of what happened was affecting me. There aren't many things I lost that I think much about, but I wish I had that ball. Glavine was my absolute favorite Brave, and to catch a ball at the World Series was thrilling.

In that same little area of my office I'd kept all my Olympic memorabilia from the 1996 Atlanta games. Dawn had made a collage for me with ticket stubs, pins, and photos from two of the most fun weeks of my life. I wish I had that as well. But like I said earlier, we were all alive and healthy and that's really all that matters. The memory of catching that World Series ball is embedded in my mind, and when I think about it, I can almost take myself back to that exact moment. They can take your stuff, but no matter what happens in life they can't take your memories.

When the fire chief arrived, we walked around to the deck to look at the grill and try to figure out what had happened. Sure enough, the knob of the grill was turned to the "off" position. A small consolation, but definitely nice to know.

Then we talked about the most likely cause of the fire. The grill was just a few inches from the house, as it had been for the last four plus years. We had grilled some delicious ribs with Dawn's homemade barbeque sauce. Instead of turning the grill off immediately, I'd left it on for about an hour to burn off the grease. Around 9:00 I turned the grill off. The chief believed that a tiny spark must have caught the wood shingle and very slowly burned up the underside of the outer shingles. Five hours or so later the fire was burning the outside of the back of our house, which created the miraculously beautiful glow that captured Dawn's attention.

That, ladies and gentlemen, is how Dawn saved Mr. Lucky's life. I am happy to report that although we lost 85 percent of our stuff, the other 15 percent included all of our photos; two Eurocaves filled with awesome wine; and the majority of our art collection, which although badly damaged, was able to be restored.

"The worst thing that's ever happened to me"

Just as we were finishing up with the fire chief, our next-door neighbor walked up to us and asked what was going on. We gave her an abbreviated version of the story. Somehow, she and her entire family had slept through five fire trucks roaring into the neighborhood and an unbelievable bonfire that brought most of the neighborhood out on the sidewalks. The only things missing were her family and the marshmallows. The first words out of her mouth were, "I can't believe I slept through this! This is the worst thing that has ever happened to me!" Happened to her? Dawn and I still laugh in astonishment at her odd response.

After this exchange, we went over to another neighbor's house for a late breakfast and to figure out what to do next. As we walked over, Melanie asked where we were going to stay. We didn't have an answer, but Mel suggested we call the Ritz-Carlton since it's very nice. It's always interesting and sometimes surprising and funny what children say or do. I was happy to know that my nine-year-old daughter had good taste, but her comment reminded us that we needed to do everything we could to ensure that she learned the value of both money and hard work. I was always thrilled when we would take her to camp and see the sign-up sheets for chores, in particular when they included things like cleaning the bathrooms.

The Biggest Shopping Spree Ever!

After breakfast we started the long process of putting our life back together. First, we found a hotel that allowed dogs. No, it wasn't the Ritz-Carlton! Next we went to the drugstore for the basics and then off to the mall to buy some clothes. If you've ever thought, "I wish I could go to the mall and buy whatever I want," let me give you the flip side to that seemingly fantastic opportunity. You have virtually nothing: no clothes, no food, no furniture. Nowhere to put any of these things. Money was not an issue, both because insurance would cover the replacement of almost everything and my business was doing well. I can guarantee you that shopping, or should I say replacing absolutely everything, will get old quickly.

Although we had virtually no possessions, we were still fortunate in so many ways. Our friends and community were amazing. When Dawn pulled up to Mel's school a couple of days later, she found an enormous pile of stuff with a sign reading "For the Epstein Family." There were pots and pans, flatware, towels, sheets, gift cards for Target and Publix, and more toilet paper than you can imagine. Hopefully it wasn't because they thought we were full of it!

Giving vs. Receiving

I joke, but as I wrote this, and almost every time I have reread the words, I tear up remembering how fabulous everyone was to us. We often found it difficult and uncomfortable to accept their generosity. We had full insurance coverage and we weren't in financial need. Why were people giving us stuff? Even people who didn't know us contributed. It reminded us that people are generally kind, thoughtful, and good, and they want to help others.

Recently we were at a small Jewish Federation of Sarasota dinner party at which a rabbi from New Orleans led a discussion about helping others versus receiving help. I said that I thought it was much easier to give than to receive. Even though everyone's heads seemed to nod in agreement, the rabbi asked why, and I had a difficult time answering. I could only think back to our fire. I think we feel vulnerable when we receive. Most of us don't want to be dependent on anyone. We also question our worthiness – whether we are worthy of people's generosity – and whether we did something wrong that put us in the situation of needing help.

The reality was that even though we would have been fine if people hadn't been so generous with us, their giving truly made things easier for us. When we moved into a house the next week, the household items proved to be useful and allowed us to assume a feeling of normalcy a little quicker. The gifts also made the givers feel helpful. I think most of us want to do something when we see someone in trouble, and even if people don't need what we give them, it makes us – the givers – feel a little less helpless.

Another lucky thing that occurred during this period was that we were able to rent a home located four houses away from ours. This house had just gone on the market after the previous renters, a terrific family from Germany with whom we had become great friends, were transferred to Sweden. When one of our neighbors told the owners of the house about our fire, they gladly took their home off the market and let us rent it for the next nine months.

Staying in the neighborhood helped us maintain some continuity in our lives and made watching over the reconstruction of our home much easier.

Everyone Wants to Help

The folks at the Wine Shop At Parkaire, where I was a regular customer, also came through for us in a big way. We were in what I would call the second stage of wine collecting. We had a EuroCave wine refrigerator in the pantry, and since I loved to buy wine almost as much as we like to drink it (Dawn says more), we had a second one in the basement. Amazingly, all the wine survived with no damage. I called the shop and told them about the fire, and hours later they showed up with boxes for 400 bottles and a truck with two guys. They stored our wines in the back of the underground portion of their building for about ten months while our house was rebuilt.

Moving back into the house was a great joy, as we were able to put the fire saga behind us. Since the structure itself was mostly intact, we ended up rebuilding our home with the same layout, except that we added a finished basement. While this might not sound exciting, I was able to incorporate a wine cellar that held a little over a thousand bottles. (The next, but not the final, stage!) I was like a kid in a candy store when my 400 bottles were delivered to the house and I got to revisit my collection.

I was recently asked about the term wine collection, which can be a bit misleading. Wine is a hobby that Dawn and I are able to enjoy together. We love to go to tastings, wine dinners, and travel to wineries, which is the best way to learn about wine. We aren't buying the wine as an investment to sell later. We are buying the wine so that in seven to twenty-plus years we'll be able to enjoy wine that has aged.

Aging the wine is the big advantage of having a collection. I'm sure there is a technical way of describing the aging process, but I'll try to keep things simple. You know how some sauces or foods taste better the next day? That's pretty much what happens with wine as the different components come together to create something magical. What's also exciting for me is remembering the place where we first discovered the wine and then experiencing it a few years later. For any number of reasons, the bottle may actually be a disappointment, but most of the time it puts a smile on our faces.

A lot of people are intimidated about wine, so I'd like to demystify it. The key thing to remember is that wine is a personal preference, so there actually is no right or wrong; it's just about discovering what you like. Try wine every chance you get, go to tastings whenever you can, and visit a winery if you have the opportunity. I'm happy to add that my doctor recommends I drink wine every day for the cancer-fighting antioxidants, so I get a lot of practice. I'm even luckier in that Dawn loves to cook, so I go into our cellar, which has over 3,000 bottles, to find something to go with her delicious meals. (We're now in stage four – the awesome and overwhelming stage where not only do you need to drink a lot of wine, but you have to have frequent parties to help manage the inventory flow!)

You Never Want to Collect on Insurance

In the midst of all this luck and generosity, there was a dark side: dealing with the insurance company, USAA. They handled our short hotel stay and the house rental efficiently and compassionately. They also treated us fairly as far as rebuilding our home. Although that process had all the usual problems, the insurance company certainly couldn't be blamed.

The big challenge was getting paid for the contents of our home. This was three years prior to the launch of the iPhone and we weren't big video people, so we didn't have photos or a video of the inside of our house. We definitely didn't have a ready catalogue of everything we owned with receipts.

There were two main issues that turned this process into hell. One was the complicated and cumbersome spreadsheet on which the insurance company required everything to be entered. I swear that this was designed to make claimants give up and save the insurer loads of money. But there was no way I was going to concede easily!

This spreadsheet claim form was probably the most significant source of tension between Dawn and me during this phase of our lives. I was determined to get the insurer to pay us every dollar that we were entitled to.

Equally challenging was the issue of how to do this without completely pissing off the fabulous person who had saved our lives. I wanted Dawn to be as diligent about the process as I was, but money wasn't, and still isn't, as important to her as it is to me. She wanted the process to be finished so we could resume our normal lives. I won't bore you with the details, let's just say I found some effective strategies to minimize leaving money on the table – and we received an adequate insurance settlement without destroying our marriage!

Be Persistent

One of my greatest strengths, which occasionally turns into a weakness, is that I am extremely persistent. When I set my mind to doing something, whether it's simple or more complex, almost nothing will stop me. To me, things like exercising more or giving up coffee are easy. If I want to do something, I just make it a priority. I find scheduling a reminder on my calendar helpful.

When I worked long hours, I found time to exercise either before work or during lunch. Working out wasn't a luxury or pleasure activity, although I did enjoy it. I consider working out like brushing your teeth or taking a shower; you exercise because it's necessary for good health. A side benefit was that I would often come up with a strategy or answer to a problem during my workout time.

I was asked recently how I became so disciplined. I believe playing sports from a young age contributed to my discipline and competitiveness. Sports provides a great opportunity to learn so many life skills, especially teamwork. I think it's phenomenal that female sports participation has increased dramatically. My niece Julia recently told me that her professors commented on how well she accepted critiques. She attributed this skill to being on the dance team since she was three years old.

Getting stuff done is just another "Nike moment" for me. Most of my life this has served me well, but at times this persistence comes across as stubbornness and has impacted relationships. Nowadays I believe that my yoga practice has had a very positive impact on me and that I am far more flexible, both physically and mentally, than I was at that time. Even so, just two years ago in the heat of a tense situation, a friend told me to stop taking myself so seriously. Wow, was that good advice! I'll write more about yoga later.

As a consultant I spent a lot of time convincing people to do something differently, which often comes across as "Your way is wrong and mine is right." I believe that in order to be effective implementing a strategy, you must have complete conviction in it. I'm not saying there is only one way to do something, or that circumstances don't change and that a strategy never needs to be modified. But it's human nature to revert to what you were already doing rather than make needed changes, so everyone has to be completely convinced and onboard. This is especially true for something that has been done a certain way for a long time.

This brings me to one of life's great lessons: Do you want to be right or do you want to be happy? One of the more difficult things for me was to recognize that even though every detail is important in business, everyday life is totally different. When someone, in particular your wife or child, says something slightly incorrect, most of the time the best thing to do is focus on what was right and ignore what was wrong. I also recognize that we make dozens of inconsequential decisions each day, and there is no reason to make a big deal or stress about them.

I have recently come to realize that the real issue for me is that I like to be in control. At a minimum I want to know that there is a plan, and of course I want to know what the plan is. Why am I sharing this information? Because understanding yourself is an essential step in becoming a happier person. And one of the qualities many of us should examine is our need for control – or the illusion that we have it.

None of us is perfect and it's unlikely we will reach perfection, if for no other reason than perfection is merely a word or concept that constantly changes. You might think you want your child, partner, or friend to be different in some way, but would you actually be happier if they made that change? Maybe a better solution is for you to understand yourself better, and then you can change your perspective.

Life Lessons from Mr. Lucky

Remember, it's only stuff.

Video your possessions.

Learn to accept the help and generosity of others.

Make sure you have good insurance from a high-quality company.

When dealing with insurance companies – be persistent.

Do you want to be right, or do you want to be happy?

Understand yourself, especially your desire for control.

CHAPTER 17

US Banking Alliance: Marketing, Service, and Integrity

I'm certainly not an expert on marketing, but I can definitely share what worked for us and what did not. As I said, speaking at conferences was our most effective way to generate high-quality leads, in particular when CEOs were in the audience. We had some success with the chief lending officers (CLOs) but almost none with the chief financial officers (CFOs). It wasn't that they didn't think we could help them, but they usually didn't have the clout relative to the CLO and CEO.

Hosting a booth at industry conferences was an effective way to generate leads when I was a presenter; however, the quality was greatly diminished when we weren't speaking. This was also expensive and time-consuming.

My philosophy regarding our website was unconventional, as I didn't believe that having a good website would help us grow faster. We had one of the least impressive websites in our field, and our booth at conferences was equally spartan. When I finally relented and upgraded our website, my objective was to spend the least amount of time and money needed, and my goal was just to have the website not suck. I wanted the site to clearly show the basics, and the only things I really cared about were having a quick demo of the software, a good description of our solution, and numerous testimonials from our clients about the value of our solution.

I won't defend this philosophy vigorously or say it's right for most companies, especially for a smaller company trying to establish a presence in today's market. We did make an effort to create meaningful content for web-blasts to our prospects, although they were never done "professionally." I will reiterate that we achieved steady client growth and strong profitability with only a minimal expenditure on marketing.

Customer Service

For the most part, I am appalled by the service I receive on a day-to-day basis. Apple is currently the most valuable company in the world with, perhaps, the most loved products, and I would rate their customer service as unsatisfactory. I have actually been frustrated enough that I have sold small amounts of Apple stock more than once because I couldn't believe how lousy their service is, and I assumed that this would eventually hurt their business. That obviously hasn't been a profitable decision!

Tim Cook, Apple's CEO, should spend some time with Howard Schultz, former CEO of Starbucks and author of many books, including *Pour Your Heart Into It*. The inspirational story of Starbucks is a must-read for anyone with entrepreneurial dreams. Starbucks doesn't always get it right, but they treat their employees well and they in turn work very hard to provide a consistently good customer experience. Who would have imagined when Schultz became CEO in 1986 that we would be spending $5 for a good, but not great, cup of coffee?

An example of a company consistently creating an exceptional customer service experience is Disney. They greet you enthusiastically when you excitedly arrive at their parks, and they thank you in a calming way when you leave, knowing that most people are exhausted. Thirty years ago, before technology changed everything, their processes were so comprehensive that if you forgot where you parked, they could help you locate your car based on the time you arrived. This level of attention to detail is what's necessary to provide an outstanding customer experience.

Why is customer service so bad, and what can be done about it? At a minimum a business has to genuinely care about its employees, have them all evaluate the company from the customer's perspective, and empower the employees to take care of customers, especially when there are problems.

I may sound somewhat skeptical and frugal regarding marketing, but I believe that providing great customer service is a sure way to grow your business. Customer service shouldn't be thought of as an expense to be reduced to make your quarterly numbers. You can't focus on customer service for a week or a month; you have to be fully committed, starting with the hiring process.

Phone service is my biggest pet peeve. I may be old school, but I was not willing to have an automated phone service at US Banking Alliance. Not only did I want someone to answer the phone when a client or prospect called, I wanted everybody to answer the phone the same way and have the same voicemail greeting. A friendly greeting from a person who is smiling as they identify themselves and the company costs next to nothing. If you insist on having an automated system, I recommend at least allowing the customer to press zero to talk to a live person. If it weren't so maddening, it would be comical how difficult some companies make it to even find their telephone numbers.

Honesty and Integrity

I haven't talked much about honesty and integrity. I believe this is another key factor at successful companies. There are so many examples of dishonesty among world leaders, corporate executives, law enforcement, and even the clergy in our society. Please try to picture me either jumping up and down or pounding the table. I can't say this strongly enough: There is nothing more critical than honesty and integrity. I don't know if the truth will set you free, but I know that in the long run, honesty pays off.

Ben Franklin said it concisely: "Honesty is the best policy." Jason Cohen, CEO of WP Engine, gave an engaging talk entitled "How Honesty Makes Money" at PrecisionLender's 2017 Bank on Purpose Conference. I highly recommend taking an hour to watch this thought-provoking, entertaining presentation.

Personally, one of the things I am most proud of is the letter I received when I retired from my friend, and our fantastic sales associate, John Whetstone. He basically said he was so proud to work for our company and that he had never worked for a person or company with such a high level of integrity.

Owning a Business – It Ain't Easy

The responsibility of owning a business energized me most of the time, but it also was a heavy burden. Granted, it was my own choosing, but unless you have owned a business, you can't truly understand the pressure. In hindsight, I know I didn't handle the responsibility with as much grace and ease as I would have liked. As the sole owner, I carried the burden with me every minute of each day. For most people, evenings, weekends, and vacations present the opportunity for rest and relaxation. Unfortunately, technology has turned many of us into 24/7 people. As an owner, you are not only checking your email but also looking over your shoulder, thinking about the competition, or planning for some new opportunity. I allowed myself little true downtime.

I have to laugh when I think about many of the conversations I've had with people wanting to start a business. They talk about making their own hours and not having to do stuff they don't want to. This may be true for some business owners, but not for any I have ever known. In my case, each year I worked more than the previous year, and at the end of the year I thought I couldn't possibly work any harder, but the next year I always did.

As for not doing things you don't want to, that may be true occasionally. But if the kitchen counter needed to be cleaned, I didn't waste time asking someone to clean it or write a memo to the staff; I just cleaned it. I was usually the first one in the office and the last person to leave. If your business is growing, there is never enough time in the day, as stuff always needs to be done. As a leader, you do your best to set an example and just do it. For the most part my team saw this, and I believe my example inspired them to work hard as well.

I don't mean to discourage anyone who wants to start their own business. I just think it's essential to have a realistic picture of what that will be like. Along with the long hours, there are plenty of missed events, family and otherwise. I was fortunate to have such a supportive wife. There were periods when I traveled so much that Dawn joked that Melanie probably wasn't sure if I was her father or Dawn's boyfriend visiting on the weekend. I often felt guilty about not spending more time with Dawn and Melanie. When Dawn recently told me that I always put them first, I was relieved and grateful to hear her perspective.

I occasionally wonder what would have happened if I had become a yogi at age eighteen or twenty-eight instead of age forty-eight. If there is any one thing that would help people living a busy life, it's yoga. Not too long ago this statement would have been considered extreme. However, Pete Carroll, head coach of the Seattle Seahawks, requires his players to do yoga and meditate, and their 2014 Super Bowl victory is an indicator of its impact. Ray Dalio, the successful investor and author I referenced earlier, says meditation is "the single most important reason" for his success.

I believe having a mentor or belonging to a group with other CEOs to discuss particular challenges and opportunities also would have been helpful.

As a sole owner you definitely control your own destiny, and the reward for success is unlimited. However, the responsibility is tremendous, so having more skills to help handle the stress would have been extremely beneficial. All this said, I am glad I finally made the decision to go out on my own.

Life Lessons from Mr. Lucky

Provide outstanding customer service.

Nothing is more critical than honesty and integrity.

Being a business owner is extremely challenging and can be very rewarding.

Learning to destress is important.

CHAPTER 18
Dad Dying

Early in the morning on Saturday, May 29, 2004, my sister Lisa received a call from my father's wife, Betty, informing her that our dad had woken up in the middle of the night convulsing. He had been taken to the hospital, where it was determined that he had suffered from a stroke caused by a brain clot, and he was scheduled to have brain surgery Tuesday morning. Since Dawn, Melanie, and I happened to be visiting my sister and her family for the Memorial Day weekend, my sister immediately woke us to deliver this devastating news.

We were all shocked, as my dad had been cancer-free for more than five years; he worked out vigorously with a personal trainer two or three times a week; and he looked terrific for a sixty-six-year-old. After an anxious couple of days, we went back to Atlanta. The next morning I flew to south Florida and met Lisa at the hospital.

I remember the two of us sitting there, nervously awaiting word from the doctors. Surgery is always a risk, but in my mind this was the big one. I have said, "It's not rocket science" or "It ain't brain surgery" many times, but this time it was, and we were very concerned. Unfortunately, the result of the surgery wasn't the miracle we hoped for, and our dad was in a coma for a few days. The doctor told us it was a good sign when my dad squeezed my sister's hand after hearing her voice.

The situation was made worse when we were informed that Betty wasn't just worried about dad's health. She had recently found out that Dad had lied to her and not changed the beneficiaries on his life insurance policy. To say that she was livid would be an understatement. The situation never got much better for my dad, although he came out of the coma. Lisa and I visited him often and he seemed to enjoy hearing stories about the family and talking about old sporting events; but his mental capacity was limited.

Don't Wait

My buddy Courtney and I talked about my dad's death recently, and he reminded me of one of the most relevant things I said to him after my dad died. I told him how thankful I was that despite everything, I had an excellent relationship with my dad. He was the best man at my wedding, and we shared many fabulous times. Most significant was that we each knew how much we loved each other and we expressed our feelings often.

You hear people talk about the meaningful discussions that they finally have with a loved one on their deathbed. These moments are special, but it's also sad that the individuals were not able to express their feelings earlier in their lives, when the impact could have been far greater.

I strongly encourage you to have that difficult conversation with a friend or loved one. Don't wait until they are on their deathbed, because the opportunity may never present itself. Even though my dad remained alive for four months, neither Lisa nor I had a substantial conversation with him during that time because of his limitations. Despite our strong relationship, this was disappointing and frustrating.

There was a short period where the family dynamics improved as we rallied for my dad. Then in typical fashion, Betty erupted once again. This time she prohibited the nursing station from giving us any information about Dad, and then went to California for three weeks. Before she left, Betty did manage to get my dad to illegibly scratch his signature on a change of insurance beneficiary form. All these years later I'm still amazed that someone would incessantly badger a person on their deathbed and do something so despicable.

The experience of seeing my dad in such a weakened state was horrible. Wondering what he was thinking and feeling with no way to meaningfully communicate made it even tougher. At one point we were seriously considering moving Dad to Atlanta or to Westerly, Rhode Island, where Lisa lived. However, there were so many obstacles, not the least of which was Betty, who more than once reminded us that we had no legal rights regarding our dad.

The scariest part of the four-month ordeal was when Ivan, a Category 5 hurricane, barreled toward south Florida, and everyone was ordered to evacuate. Only the bare minimum of hospital staff and emergency crew remained behind to protect people like my dad, who had no one looking out for him. Lisa and I had talked with Dad about his marriage and his decision to stick it out many times. Until then, none of us ever envisioned a worst-case scenario like my dad dying while floating down the street. Talk about feeling helpless.

Saying Goodbye

The saddest moment came shortly after we were told that Dad had been transferred into the hospice ward. Lisa and I quickly went to Florida for one last visit. We didn't know how long he would be there before he passed, of course, but we definitely did not want to be by his bedside with Betty, who had returned from California. We were able to meet at the hospital with Dad's rabbi and his best friend, Stewart. They both visited Dad regularly and had helped us throughout the ordeal.

On this particular day the rabbi led us in a quick prayer, and then we said our final goodbye to Dad. Lisa and I both remember the surreal feeling of walking down the hall, knowing that we would never see our father again. Thankfully we had each other, then and always. As we returned home to wait for the inevitable call letting us know that Dad had passed, we probably should have known that things would get even worse between us and Betty, but we didn't.

The night before we headed back to Florida for the funeral, my Aunt Carole called to let us know that Betty had informed her that we were not welcome to sit Shiva, a Jewish ritual following burial, at my dad's house. In hindsight this was probably a blessing, and we quickly made alternative plans. I am happy to say that except for seeing her from a distance at the funeral and the cemetery, I have not seen or spoken to her again.

Lisa was not as fortunate, as Betty showed up at her deposition regarding the change in Dad's insurance policy. Yes, you read that correctly (details momentarily). Our wonderful father, who we remember lovingly, provided another lesson for us all. In his will, he had designated his wife as the person to distribute all of his personal items. Even in the best of circumstances, this seems like a bad idea, and this certainly wasn't the best of circumstances. He was fully aware of the soured relationship between his wife and his children, so his decision was guaranteed to lead to strife following his death.

Family First

What happened with the insurance policy was that my sister and I went from a substantial portion of the proceeds to an insignificant amount. This left Lisa and me with an extremely difficult decision as to whether to file a lawsuit against Betty. The case seemed simple enough on the surface: My dad had brain surgery and his mental capacity was severely compromised. His distinctive signature on the previous insurance designation was replaced by an illegible scribble on the document that he "signed" while he was in the hospital.

Dawn and I discussed the situation and decided we did not want to spend the time and energy fighting this battle, but we knew that the money was meaningful for my sister and her family. We thought, as a compromise, we would give Lisa the money ourselves. She and her husband Marcus greatly appreciated the gesture but felt the principle of the situation was the most significant factor.

We probably all would have walked away from the situation, no matter how we felt about Betty, if we believed they had been happy together. But she mostly made Dad's life hell, with one exception. She took good care of him each time he was ill or in the hospital until this final episode.

As much as I didn't want to be involved in the lawsuit, I would do anything for my sister. We spent the next eighteen months working with an attorney, hoping that our father's real intention would be carried out. To make a long, sorry story short, when we finally got to the stage where we would have to go to court for the trial, Lisa couldn't imagine being in the courtroom with Betty. We called our attorney and settled the case, with the majority of the money going to the attorneys and Betty in exchange for a few personal items of our dad's.

As Lisa and I recently reflected about the lawsuit, we tried to imagine what we would tell our best friend to do if they were in the exact same situation. In our case, the choice to legally address the situation led to frustration, anger, and sadness, and ultimately the result was mostly unfavorable. What we don't know is how we would have felt if we had walked away and let Betty have everything.

Regardless, we have the most meaningful thing that you can have in life. We have a strong, loving relationship that has helped us through life's many challenges, and our two families share virtually all of life's most special times together.

Life Lessons from Mr. Lucky

Communicate your love and appreciation at every opportunity.

Don't wait to address difficult issues.

Ensure that your will and estate documents are as thoughtful and complete as possible.

CHAPTER 19
Do You Know How Much Your Company is Worth?

I was in Carl Ryden's office, telling him what his 2005 year-end bonus would be, when he asked me about my exit plan for the company. I told him that I'd never thought about it – that I just focused on delivering for our clients and had no plans for selling the business. And I meant it! I told him that I assumed, someday, someone would give me a call and ask me to go to lunch or something. This might sound naïve, but I literally never spent any time thinking about selling the company.

I don't think Carl laughed at me – that's not his style – but he told me that was not how it worked. He also asked me if I had any idea how much the company was worth. I knew that the business was doing great. Personally, I was making a lot of money and I was able to pay my people well, including providing them with generous bonuses. That said, I had no idea what the business was worth. I had never had even a quick discussion about the value of the company with anyone.

Carl showed me a simple spreadsheet that he had created with a few assumptions. I found it interesting to say the least. Actually, my reaction was probably more like shock. If Carl was right, I would never have to work again and my family would be financially secure. What was equally significant to me was that the people to whom I had given equity participation rights in the event of a company sale would all receive consequential sums of money.

I actually don't remember much about what came next. I do know that even though the business was more successful in terms of sales and profitability every single year, I wasn't enjoying it much anymore. I derived the most satisfaction from the consulting aspect of the business – helping the clients – but I was no longer doing this. I think I'd only spent one week that year with a client actually doing what I loved. The only reason I went onsite for that job was because it was a bigger client, and they insisted they wouldn't hire us any other way.

I was still working and traveling as much as I had before, but my travel primarily involved speaking at industry conferences. When I wasn't doing that, I was running the business. The worst part was managing the people. I liked all the people. Or to be more accurate, I liked everyone most of the time! We were like family, so I knew many of their personal problems. I even lent one of them a pretty significant amount of money to get out of a jam. I definitely struggled with this and the petty stuff that occasionally occurred between employees. I often joked with Dawn that if it weren't for the employees, my job would have been fantastic.

Another factor I considered as I decided whether to sell the business was my father's situation. As I said earlier, he'd lost 90 percent of his wealth when the dot-com bubble burst. I knew I did not want to make the same mistake as my dad. In hindsight, putting a business up for sale in the summer of 2006 was brilliant, but I can assure you this was just the gods looking out for Mr. Lucky.

My Doctor Said

I also thought about the short conversations I had with my doctor during my annual physical. He would do all the typical doctor things, poking and prodding places that weren't any fun. Then he would ask me a little about my family life, my business, and what my number was. At first I wasn't sure what he was asking, but he wanted to know how much money I thought I needed before I had enough. This wasn't anything I was focused on, but I found it interesting that a doctor would ask about this.

The most impactful thing my doctor told me was that most successful business owners he had as patients ended up with either heart attacks or divorces. Both of these were situations I wanted to avoid! He always got me thinking, which I greatly appreciate, and he genuinely seemed to care about me rather than trying to scare me.

The last factor I considered, although not with much intensity, was what would be necessary to take the business to the next level. As you grow a business from $1 million in revenue to $5 million to $10 million, etc., different skill sets are needed. Looking back through my career, I recognized I had a limited background. I knew banking well and I was an expert in loan and deposit pricing, but prior to going out on my own, I had never managed more than two employees, and in 2006 our company totaled only fifteen people. Over the past few years I had learned a lot about marketing and sales from reading books and attending the school of hard knocks. But would this be enough?

Clearly, we were a highly profitable company that had strong margins and a growing, recurring revenue base with totally satisfied clients. The competition still did not have an offering anywhere close to what we had. The biggest risk to our business was that one of the big core processors would develop good loan pricing software.

Bankers like to get as many products as possible from the same provider, and most banks have a core processor that provides the basic system of record for a bank. If one of them developed a product that was "good enough," even if not superior ours, they would be able to bundle it with other products and become a much more formidable competitor.

In the end I decided I couldn't go wrong selling my business if someone was willing to pay me handsomely for it. I'll never know if I was capable of taking the business to the next level, but I have zero regret for not sticking around to find out. I think the main factor that allowed me to be comfortable with my decision is that I don't have a big ego. I am realistic about what I bring to the table as well as my limitations. That said, I think it's virtually impossible to be successful without a high level of confidence in your ability, and I was confident in mine.

During my business career I have encountered many people who thought too much of themselves. I believe most people would benefit from regularly assessing their strengths and weaknesses and creating a career game plan. Few people enjoy their annual review, but this can definitely be a good place to start. You make errors in judgment when you think you're smarter than you are, and the result can be serious when your career is involved. It might not have been catastrophic for my business if I had thought it could have been the next billion-dollar company and that I was the right person to lead us there. But I probably wouldn't have sold the business when I did; and since the great recession hit two years later, at a minimum, times would have been a lot tougher.

Chipper Jones and the Atlanta Braves

I'll use a Chipper Jones story to illustrate how ego can get the better of you and then get back to the story of selling US Banking Alliance and the disastrous mistakes that our purchaser made. Have I mentioned Mr. Lucky's amazing timing deciding in May of 1991 to purchase Atlanta Braves season tickets? From 1985 to 1990, America's team finished in last place four times and in next-to-last place twice.

April of 1991 was not much better, but I had a feeling that the Braves were about to turn the corner, and I have never been more correct with any decision except the one to marry Dawn Minette Wishnie. In July of 1991, the Braves trailed the Dodgers by nine and a half games. And then they went on a tear, capping their "Worst to First" season with a trip to the World Series. The astonishing run ended when Jack Morris outdueled John Smoltz in the tenth inning of a 1-0 Minnesota Twins victory in Game 7 of the World Series.

The magic continued in 1992, culminating with the spectacular slide into home by Sid Bream in Game 7 of the National Championship series, just ahead of Barry Bonds's throw to the plate. The Braves literally caught fire in July of 1993. Two hours before the start time on the day they acquired Fred "Crime Dog" McGriff, the press box went up in flames. Although the game was delayed by two hours, that night was the start of a 51-17 run that catapulted the Braves to a third straight division title en route to making the playoffs fourteen seasons in a row.

Dawn and I were able to attend all home playoff and World Series games during the entire stretch. There wasn't anything more fun than Game 6 of the 1995 World Series, as the Braves beat the Cleveland Indians 1-0 behind Tom Glavine's two-hit, eight-inning masterpiece and David Justice's game-winning home run. (A close second was two weeks before, when we had gone to the first-ever Florida Gators vs. Georgia Bulldogs football game played in Athens, Georgia. The Steve Spurrier-led Gators hung "half a hundred" on the Dogs for the first time ever in their own stadium. Then we zipped over to Fulton County Stadium for the final game of the National League Championship series, where the Braves beat the Reds 6-0 to complete a four-game sweep. What a day of sports!)

Say Thank You

Shortly after their World Series victory, we met Chipper Jones at an Atlanta Falcons game. There were sixteen of us sitting in a luxury box. Dawn waited until halftime to introduce herself to Chipper and excitedly told him that we were Braves season ticket holders. He remarked that we were very lucky. She then asked to see his World Series ring, which he held out as he looked away. I mentioned that there were only sixteen people in the box because I want to be clear that he hadn't been getting pestered all afternoon, and we were obviously all friends of the host. I should also add that my wife is a pretty lady.

Why couldn't Chipper have thanked her for being a season ticket holder or mentioned how passionate and supportive the fans were or done something to make her feel good about the quick exchange? From that point on, I don't think Dawn ever cheered for Chipper again, even after he would hit a game-winning home run.

Chipper was right in saying that we were lucky to have the opportunity to see arguably the best pitching staff of all time with three future Hall of Famers: Tom Glavine, John Smoltz, and Greg Maddux.

Although it clearly didn't impact his career, why do people like Chipper get so full of themselves? He didn't come up with the cure for cancer. He is now in the Baseball Hall of Fame, so he is clearly among the best at what he did. However, he is no better than you or me. As the saying goes, we all put our pants on one leg at a time.

You are definitely not better than others because you make more money. My advice is to be the best, whether you are a teacher, a nuclear physicist, the trash collector, or whatever you are doing to earn an honest living. And equally important, make sure you treat everybody in the world with respect.

Life Lessons from Mr. Lucky

Your health is everything.

Be confident but realistic.

Regularly assess your strengths and weaknesses.

Check your ego at the door.

"Thank you" is a simple phrase with high value.

Treat everyone with respect.

Be the best you can be at what you do and who you are.

CHAPTER 20
Selling the Business

Since this was my first rodeo, I was happy to have Carl take the lead once I made the decision to put the business up for sale. The most essential part of the process was getting the right team in place. Carl interviewed several investment bankers over the phone and narrowed the long list down to three. We then met with Robinson Humphries, a division of SunTrust Bank, out of Atlanta; Marks Baughan (MB), a boutique firm from Philadelphia; and a mid-size firm out of Memphis.

We chose MB for two reasons. First, they only worked with technology firms in the financial industry and knew all the players who were likely to be interested in buying the company. Because of the unique nature of US Banking Alliance, none of the investment bankers was very certain how much money the company was worth. However, MB offered an attractive fee structure. Their fees were relatively in line with the others, but if the price was on the low end, their fee would be reduced considerably. If it was above a certain threshold, their percentage would continue to increase with the sales price. I really liked this structure, as I knew MB's interests would be aligned with ours.

The other parts of our team included our accounting firm and a law firm. When I met with my attorney to let him know that I was ready to explore selling the company he was excited for me, as he had helped me negotiate the earn-out agreement to purchase my business in the first place. He was surprised that things had gone so well. He said earn-out structures often get ugly, and he had feared that the people I did my original deal with would try to make some kind of claim on my business, given the success.

As much as I hated to, I chose a different law firm. I was totally satisfied with the first attorney's work; but his firm typically only worked on one or two merger and acquisition deals a year. Anybody who was likely to buy us would have a more experienced legal team.

The original firm would probably have done an excellent job and been dramatically less expensive, but this was the biggest, most significant financial transaction of my life. The most likely scenario was that this would be the one and only significant transaction in my life. This was not the time to try to save money. I definitely needed a highly experienced team. In hindsight, our decision to hire Morris, Manning & Martin LLP was crucial.

The first time we bought a house I remember being nervous while signing the mountain of boilerplate legal documents. This was a much more significant transaction with an endless number of items that needed to be negotiated. I can't tell you how many times the buyer said "This is the standard" or "This is the typical way to handle it" about some key aspect of the deal. Many of these times my attorney or someone on my investment banker's team said that was not the case, and they were able to back it up, as they were both extremely experienced. When you add all these things up, we're talking about real money. Even more crucial, when we started another business these negotiated items protected us from legal issues – something I never anticipated.

Finding a Buyer

Once the deal team was in place, we focused on putting together a two-page teaser for the investment banker to send to anyone who might be a prospective buyer. Those who were interested signed a nondisclosure agreement (NDA) and were given the deal book, which is a fairly detailed look at the company. Preparing the deal book is another time-consuming part of the process, as you want to portray your company both as accurately and as favorably as possible to get the highest value.

No matter how certain you are about whom the likely buyers are, you want to cast a wide net to create as much interest as possible and hopefully a bidding war. Buyers are divided into two groups: strategic buyers and financial buyers. Strategic buyers are companies in similar or closely related businesses. Financial buyers, like private equity companies, are typically looking to invest in the business primarily for financial gain.

I made the decision not to let anyone in the company know about my determination to sell the business except my executive assistant, Laurie, whom I trusted with everything, and Carl. My reasoning was pretty simple. The process was expected to take approximately six months and be time-consuming and stressful as the deal ebbed and flowed. There was also the possibility that there would be no transaction. Equally crucial was that I needed to make sure the business continued to do well so that at no point in the process, especially the final stages, could the buyer push the price down.

As companies expressed interest and signed the NDA, Carl and I did webcast presentations with serious buyers. This allowed them to gain additional insight into our business and for both groups to get an initial feel for one another. I was totally comfortable selling via webcast, as I had been doing four or five a week for the last three or four years. I wouldn't say that I was nervous, but I was certainly aware that the stakes were escalated.

I am also confident in saying that we answered each question as accurately as possible. Integrity is the most critical personal attribute you can have. Someone may not agree with me, or like what I say or do, but I am an honest person and you can count on my word, whether we are playing a card game for bragging rights or selling a company for serious money.

Carl and I quickly got in a groove. A fair number of folks were interested in buying the company, but many of the preliminary indications of interest were at levels that I didn't consider very attractive. Fortunately we had one strategic buyer, Jack Henry & Associates, that was highly interested early on, and their initial valuation was strong. What we needed was at least one other serious group.

Over the next month two more companies expressed a good level of interest, one a strategic buyer and one a financial buyer. The next step was to meet in person with the three companies so that each side could drill down and continue to size each other up. At this point I brought the senior consultants up to date on what was going on. They were excited, as they had stock appreciation rights (SARs) that would provide them a share of the proceeds if a sale occurred. They were also somewhat anxious, as no one truly knew what this meant for the day-to-day business after a sale.

The consultants were mostly skeptical of the financial buyer, as it was a private equity (PE) firm. None of us except Carl had much knowledge about PEs beyond their reputation for cutting costs and doing things strictly focused on getting value from an acquisition. To my mind the consultants' concerns about PE didn't have much validity, as we only had fifteen employees and we were highly profitable; their jobs were certainly safe.

I have gotten to know some PE firms fairly well in the last five years and I have seen both sides. Yes, there can certainly be the sleaze factor, as they are focused on getting returns for their shareholders. However, the good ones have an endless amount of management experience, connections, and know how to add tremendous value to an acquisition. Private equity is no different than any other profession or group of people, be it bankers, politicians, doctors, lawyers, husbands/wives, the clergy, etc.; there are many good ones and some bad ones.

As a society, we would be a lot better off if we got to know one another, as opposed to quickly judging or labeling each other. Most of us are good people, and we have more in common than what divides us. Sadly, fewer and fewer people seem interested in hearing the other side's view and working together.

Make Me an Offer I Can't Refuse

After the face-to-face meetings, things got serious as the time for submitting a written letter of intent approached. In the end we received only one offer. Happily, the offer came from Jack Henry, the strategic buyer that had been interested from the start, and their bid was attractive.

The tricky part of negotiating the price was that there was only one bidder. The good news was that the bidder definitely wanted us and didn't know that they were the only one. Jim Marks, the lead partner at MB, explained to me that we needed to tread extremely carefully during the price negotiation. We absolutely didn't want to scare them off. At the same time, there would be lots of things to negotiate besides price. If they knew that we had no backup, they could walk all over us during the entire process.

Carl and I didn't share this information with anyone. In fact, thirteen years later this is the first time I have mentioned it. I'm pleased to say that Jim was able to get them to raise their offer one time before we agreed on the price.

Aside from price, we were also thrilled because the buyer seemed to be a perfect fit. They were the third-largest bank data processing company, so they had a good market position. They had a separate division of fifteen companies they had purchased, and we would be able to leverage their sales and marketing. More importantly, they could bundle products and create a suite of solutions that would position us for years to come. Both organizations saw this as the Holy Grail for our clients, as bankers wanted fewer vendors and fewer disparate solutions.

We connected well with their executive team. They seemed eager for us to share our sales processes, our delivery methodology, and our customer service approach with the other fifteen previously purchased companies, as we were far more profitable than any of them.

At this stage both parties signed a letter of intent. Over the next sixty days, they would examine every last aspect of US Banking Alliance's financial documents, reports, processes, and talk to our employees and clients to make certain of what they were buying. Simultaneously, we would negotiate a purchase agreement. As I mentioned, we needed to make sure that we kept the business growing, just as we projected in our deal book and all of our conversations with them.

For the most part, things went reasonably well with the negotiation and due diligence process. This basically means that although we encountered many sticky issues, neither side got close to walking on the deal.

And Then Things Got Stupid

In the final stages of the process, the buyer said to me that my senior consultants didn't fit into their salary structure, as they were making too much money. I was shocked that this was an issue. I reminded them that they were buying us because we had a great product that we packaged with excellent consulting services, we had a 97 percent client retention rate, and we were highly profitable – even given our employees' salaries, which they clearly earned.

They also told me that they didn't believe in bonuses, which I had been paying to reward the team for our success. Did I mention our strong profitability? How can I say this politely; they were missing the big picture!

Just to be clear, the consultants were well paid, but I obviously didn't think they were overpaid. They played a key role in our success, and I did my best to fully convey the uniqueness of their skill set. That said, I decided that this wouldn't be a productive argument as there was no way to prove whether or not they were overpaid.

The crucial question was how the buyer thought these issues could best be addressed. Their answer was that I needed to let the consultants know that after closing, their salaries would be cut significantly and their bonuses would be eliminated. I didn't think this strategy would go over well but, hey, what did I know? This was my first deal and their sixteenth. They didn't think this would be a big issue, since the consultants would all be getting significant sums of money as part of the transaction.

To be sure I had this straight and was prepared when I met with each of my consultants, I asked the buyer if they were sure this was the way they wanted to begin their relationship with these guys. They said it was.

I met with each of the consultants and tried to put lipstick on this pig, pointing out that they were going to be getting large payouts if the deal closed. Surprisingly, it turned out I was right; they all thought this was a *big* FKN deal! They couldn't believe that the first club out of the buyer's bag was to cut their salary – *and* eliminate their bonuses. The consultants believed that the money they would receive from the sale reflected the value that they had helped create – period, end of story. Their future compensation had nothing to do with what they received from the transaction. Who were these people who didn't recognize their value going forward? I completely agreed with the consultants.

If you think cutting their pay was stupid, wait until you hear about our employment contracts. The buyer insisted that the three senior consultants, as well as Carl and I, sign employment contracts, which were for two years. There was nothing atypical about wanting to lock in the key players in a deal like this. What *was* highly unusual were the terms of the employment agreements.

The agreement basically gave the employer the right to end each of our employment contracts for any or no particular reason. Here is the biggie! The agreement gave each of us the exact same right. Yes, you read that correctly. Any of us could leave the company at any time we wanted. Yes, we had to sign non-compete clauses and confidentiality agreements, but any, or all, of us, could leave whenever we wanted.

I also had to address the fact that the buyer didn't believe in bonuses with the rest of the staff. There was nothing fun about that, as most of them were used to getting a 25 percent bonus. The buyer was more reasonable on this issue, as they were willing to give all of these employees a 10 to 15 percent raise, effective at the close. Since the deal was expected to close on November 1st, the staff also received a bonus at close for the first ten months of the year with US Banking Alliance. That said, everybody wondered about this company that didn't want to incent them, and they probably sensed that the consultants didn't seem happy.

I was able to convince the consultants that it made sense for us all to do the deal with Jack Henry, and if they weren't happy they could leave and get another job. In other words, they would have the opportunity to prove to the buyer that they weren't overpaid.

Stupid Leads to Crazy

The deal was set to close on November 1st. I needed to have all of the employment agreements, non-competes, and confidentiality agreements signed the day before the closing so they could be part of the closing package. Sometime the day before closing, Joel Rosenberg, the consultant who had been with me since the beginning, told me that he had a problem. He was supposed to sign and date the agreement, but the document itself had the next day's date, and there was a clause in the agreement that addressed integrity. Joel feared that by signing the employment agreement and dating it October 31st, he could be in violation of the agreement.

The rest of us had all signed the agreements, and I could not understand his concern. None of us had a problem signing and dating the agreement a day early that clearly would become *effective* on November 1st. Nor did we think that the buyer was craftily setting us all up to be in violation of our agreements right from the top. Joel was a graduate of Rensselaer Polytechnic Institute (RPI) and he was a lot smarter than I was, but holy smokes, the day before closing wasn't the time to go brain-dead.

On the day I first told the consultants about the deal, they were all totally jazzed about how much money they were going to get (it was a lot of money, especially relative to the salary impact), and they were all appreciative. They certainly had a right to be pissed about the salary issue, but I felt that at some point they needed to get over it and they didn't. I also had to handle the day-to-day running of our business and the normal deal minutiae, so by this time I was quite stressed.

Joel's stonewalling was even more challenging, as I couldn't understand the logic of his position. He told me he wasn't able to reach his attorney and he wasn't going to sign the agreement until his concern got cleared up. I reiterated that the rest of us had signed the agreement and that this was the only issue outstanding on our end. I tried again to reassure him that the date wasn't an issue; he was just misinterpreting the purpose of the integrity clause.

I was so frustrated I could not see straight. I went to Carl's office to give him this unbelievable update and talk the issue through. I also called my attorney, who offered to talk with Joel as well. Both of them told me that overall things had gone smoothly, and that this minor glitch would get worked out. Sound advice for sure, but that did nothing to give me comfort. All I could think about was how crazy it was. I certainly didn't think about how stressed Joel himself might be, or that his anxiety was playing itself out in a last-minute panicky resistance to the deal.

At some point Carl put things in perspective for Joel. He knew Joel was worried about what the new owner would do to him if he "improperly" signed the deal. Carl asked Joel to imagine what he thought the working environment would be if he didn't sign the agreement, and he was the reason that the deal didn't close.

Somehow, realizing how his actions might affect everyone else seemed to do the trick for Joel. To my relief, sometime around 9:00 pm he signed the documents, and the deal closed the next day without a hitch.

Life Lessons from Mr. Lucky

When approaching a major transaction, assemble the most qualified team you can, as mistakes can be very costly.

Avoid judging and labeling individuals, companies, and professions. Most are good – a few aren't.

When you are very stressed, recognize it's likely that others are as well.

Rise above negatives with compassion and kindness whenever possible.

CHAPTER 21

Sitting on Top
of the World

W hat can I say about my incredibly talented, funny, kind-hearted, and maddening brother-in-law, Eric Wishnie? Long before he died on July 30, 2007, at forty-five years old, I had a picture of him with Muhammad Ali in my office. Muhammad Ali, how cool is that? The champ lit the torch at the 1996 Olympic Games in Atlanta – a perfect choice. He was the greatest, floating like a butterfly and stinging like a bee, and Eric was just as amazing.

Eric started at NBC as a page and worked his way up to Senior Producer on the NBC Nightly News for Tom Brokaw, and then Brian Williams. He not only met and produced pieces about virtually all the world leaders, as well as the Michael Jordans, Warren Buffetts, and Steven Spielbergs of the world, but he made an impact on many of them as well. I wish he could have appreciated how much he meant to so many people.

Eric received the prestigious Edward R. Murrow Award, three National Emmy awards, and the Overseas Press Club Award, among his many accolades. He was a passionate Gator fan and was recognized by the University of Florida as one of their Alumni of Distinction in 2004. He was a diehard

Yankees fan who even occasionally sat in the owners' box, and he loved his dog, Lincoln.

His family, friends, and co-workers treasured every minute they had with him. Everybody loved Eric. He was a fascinating storyteller with a terrific sense of humor. He was someone who seemed to have it all; no one knew how troubled he was. We would go for long stretches without seeing or hearing from him, and then we would get together, catch up, and have a wonderful visit. He would promise that we would get together again soon, though that didn't happen. We would be disappointed and occasionally angry at Eric, but as soon as we saw him, we would forget about his broken promises to stay in touch. He was so lovable and charming that it was impossible to stay mad at him.

What went wrong with Eric is difficult to say, and Dawn knows that there is nothing she could have done to prevent his suicide. Still there was a long period when she wished that she had said and done things differently. I too have wondered what I could have done that might have made a difference in Eric's life. Dawn says yoga helped her to work through the heartbreak and forgive herself, and she believes that everyone lives the life they were meant to live.

Dawn also told me a story about a trip we made to the Upper Peninsula four years ago to visit our Sarasota neighbors, Jim and Nancy, who have a summer home there. We were returning home from a delicious dinner, feeling pretty buzzed from a lot of wine and listening to some classic rock, which made Dawn think about Eric, who loved music. Dawn heard Eric tell her not to be so sad when she thought about him, which gave her great comfort and was a crucial part of her healing process.

The concept of a dead person communicating with Dawn is something I would have been highly skeptical of several years earlier. In fact, I can still remember one night in 2001 or 2002 when I saw Dawn reading a book on past lives and reincarnation. I consider myself a fact-based realist, so these concepts were totally foreign and frankly unbelievable to me. Dawn and I met in an economics class at the University of Florida, where she graduated with a finance degree. At one time she was skeptical of these concepts as well, but after reading these books she grew open to all possibilities. I think it's fair to say that in addition to being highly skeptical, I was rude, mocking the entire concept.

About five years ago I read a truly inspirational book, *Dying to Be Me* by Anita Moorjani, that describes the author's near-death experience and recovery from four years of terminal cancer. The book changed my viewpoint about what I know and don't know about life and is another thing that has helped me to become more open-minded. I have recommended the book to a number of people with the note that whether you believe the premise or not, you will find the optimistic message very powerful.

In Eric's autobiography, written when he was thirteen, he wrote, "I will try to give and care as much as I can and I'll try to make my stay on this planet a worthwhile one." And he did. When Eric gave his funny, thoughtful speech to the University of Florida School of Journalism in 2001, his advice was "to work hard, say yes a lot (when no one else wants to), and have a little faith." His unlikely twenty-plus year journey with his dream company – which started slowly as a page in NYC and then basically a gofer in the Washington Bureau – is a good reminder of what one can achieve with hard work, a can-do attitude, and loyalty, and should serve as an inspiration to anyone. As much as I don't understand about Eric's life and death, the one thing I'm sure of is that we are alive, and the biggest tragedy would be to not fully live our lives.

After watching many friends deal with their own personal tragedies, I've learned that everybody handles devastating loss differently, and as much as we want to help, the best thing we can do is respect each other's right to grieve in our own way. No matter how hard it is to see family and friends struggle, all we can really do is let them know that we are here for them when they are ready.

Another powerful lesson is to recognize that you never truly know what is going on with others around you, even family and friends. Tom Brokaw, who at Eric's Life Celebration referred to him as "the most winning person I ever met," offered these similar thoughts: "Watch out for each other, constantly; be aware that demons lurk where laughter reigns;" and "Even our jolliest friends have more demons than they may realize."

One of the best pieces of advice I read recently was that when someone, whether you know them or not, is unkind, rude, or acts in an aggressive or disappointing way toward you, give them the benefit of the doubt. Assume their action has nothing to do with you because it probably doesn't. Then, if anything, show them extra love or compassion. Let's be part of the solution and make this world a kinder, gentler place.

Life Lessons from Mr. Lucky

There is a lot we don't know about life.

Be openminded.

Give and care as much as possible.

Say yes a lot.

Live your life fully.

Watch out for others, constantly.

Give people the benefit of the doubt.

It's not always about you.

Help make the world a kinder, gentler place.

CHAPTER 22
After the Sale

D espite the challenges associated with the closing, I was determined to do everything I could to help Jack Henry over the next two years. I relished the opportunity to take what had been my company to the next level as a division of their company. I hoped that things would settle down with the team, and that since this was a much bigger company, new opportunities would arise for some of them as a result. Equally important to me was making this transition a positive one for our clients.

I quickly found out that although many of our clients were happy for me, most of them had had negative experiences with big companies taking over smaller companies that made products they liked, and in most cases the clients ended up worse off. None of my clients were optimistic that this would be any different. I assured them that I wasn't going anywhere and that I would do everything I could to ensure that they continued to get tremendous value from our solution. I confidently stated that there would be many additional opportunities to expand and improve our solution as well.

I absolutely meant every word I said. In fact, I was so committed to doing my part that two months later I didn't go to the 2006 National Championship Football game, which included my Gators, because it would interfere with a relatively standard management call in which I was supposed to participate. Despite Ohio State's Ted Ginn running the opening kickoff back for a touchdown, Florida destroyed the Buckeyes 41-14. (Not only was this one of the most fun victories, but little did I know that the win would become even sweeter, as less than two years later we would be living in Sarasota, which is full of Buckeye fans!)

In April I put the company first again as the Gator basketball team won the National Championship, making the University of Florida the only school to win the National Championship in football and basketball during the same school year. I sat in the seventh row, right behind Patrick Ewing, for the Gators' 76-66 victory over UCLA in the semi-final game. Two nights later I wanted to go to the championship game. Instead I flew to Missouri for a company function and watched the Gators beat the Buckeyes 84-75 on a thirteen-inch TV.

My optimism turned out to be misplaced, and my clients' previous experience played out just as they had cautioned me. Jack Henry had another product with a component that did some basic but limited loan pricing. At the first division presidents' meeting, we talked about how we should handle selling these two products. I thought this discussion should have been simple; their product was vastly inferior to ours.

I was flabbergasted that we actually spent time debating the merits of their product versus ours. I strongly stated two things that were indisputable. Banks that wanted a loan-pricing solution chose our much-higher-cost product 95 percent of the time. More importantly, Jack Henry had just paid a lot of money to buy our company because they didn't have a good loan-pricing solution. That should have been the end of the story.

I have already admitted that there are times when I'm not patient even in retirement, and I definitely was not a patient person during my business career. I subscribe to the "Say what you mean, so that I can understand what you're saying" rule. That way, there is no guessing or misunderstanding about what you've said. I'm not talking about being an a-hole or disrespectful; I'm just saying that speaking honestly and directly is the best way to communicate.

The way the people at this meeting tiptoed around the facts would have been comical if I hadn't found it so frustrating. The attendees included thirteen or fourteen group presidents, all senior people who had sold their companies to Jack Henry. Presumably we were all grownups. Our boss, the person who had negotiated the purchase of each of our companies, should have spoken up immediately and stated that whenever a prospect was interested in loan pricing, our solution would be offered. Despite my comments and my clear frustration that didn't happen.

Shortly after this fun meeting, we started the budget process. At the first budget meeting, I learned that more than half of the other products were unprofitable and others were marginally profitable. I had been led to believe that Jack Henry was highly interested in me sharing some of our companies different, more profitable approaches.

The budget meetings confirmed to me that this was a big, bureaucratic organization. They didn't seem to want to make changes, and if they did, it certainly wasn't at a pace at which I wanted to operate.

Flying in a Private Plane – WOW

It should tell you something that the highlight of my time with Jack Henry wasn't about the work, the product, or the clients. Right after the close of the deal I flew in the company's private plane from Peachtree Dekalb airport to their headquarters in Monett, Missouri. There is nothing like the ease of flying private.

Unfortunately, I find it claustrophobic to be in close quarters when there is no way out and I have zero control of the situation. Shortly after boarding the plane I started getting that uncomfortable feeling. I immediately called my wife, who talked me through a breathing exercise until we lost cell connection. Ten years later my yoga practice has taught me the power of the breath to help deal with life's challenging situations.

If you have left the room to get a violin to play for the pitiful rich guy, I am telling you this story for a couple of reasons. We have all seen the spectacular private planes in the movies. I can't imagine what those are like and how much they cost, although I'm sure it would be crazy fun to ride on one. The few private planes I have flown on cost around $5,000 an hour, and you can't even stand up in them. So even though I can afford to fly private and my wife thinks we should, I can't imagine spending $10,000 or more when I can usually get two commercial tickets for less than $1,000. Dawn and I fly economy comfort as much or more than we fly first class. I love nice things and have plenty of them, but I worked way too hard to make our money, and I don't like to waste it.

You've probably figured out that I found working for a big company frustrating. As the CEO of my own company for the previous six years, I ran the show and the show moved quickly. When we had an issue, I got people's input, we analyzed things, and we immediately made decisions. Then we executed what we'd decided, analyzed the impact, tweaked things further as necessary, and moved forward again. The fifteen years before that hadn't been quite as dynamic, but they were entrepreneurial as well.

I wasn't just frustrated at Jack Henry, it was worse. I didn't feel I was making a difference or that I was needed. I found it difficult to watch them do almost nothing to enhance the solution or maximize the value of the acquisition of US Banking Alliance.

Dawn and I talked about my alternatives, including leaving. Up until that point I don't think I had ever quit anything in my life, but I definitely had to consider it. On one hand, I had said I would do everything I could to help the new owner for the next two years, and keeping my word was important to me. On the other, Jack Henry had dictated the terms of my two-year employment agreement, and it explicitly stated that either the company or I could end the agreement at any point, for any or no reason. I quickly came to a decision that I thought was totally reasonable.

I told my boss I didn't feel I was adding value to their company and I believed I had shared everything with them that they needed to make the acquisition of US Banking Alliance successful. I also said that, while there was no way I was going to continue working for the company the entire two years, I would be willing to stay a little longer. This would ensure that if there were other things they felt they needed from me, we could address them. My boss wasn't happy but didn't really have a choice. We settled on an additional six months, which I believe was more than fair. Most critically, I would be able to look at myself in the mirror, knowing that I had done the right thing for both the company and myself.

The word that best describes my state of mind at work for the next six months, in particular the last few weeks, was bored. I would do the little work I had and then shut my door so no one could see me surfing the Internet. Time seemed to move slower and slower every day.

I hope I haven't described how you feel on a typical workday; but because of that experience I developed empathy for all the people who don't enjoy their jobs. My advice is to remember that you have total control of your life and do something to change your situation. No matter what stage of your career, you can learn new skills by taking a class, reading a few books, or watching some Ted Talks. Even if you love your job, doing these things is beneficial.

Looking Back

For the most part, things settled down once the deal closed. John, my sales guy who was our highest-paid employee, retired as planned. He did his best to create a smooth transition of his pipeline for the Jack Henry team, but they didn't have the work ethic, incentive, and sales skills to maximize the opportunities. The only consultant who left the company was Courtney, who resigned three months after the deal closed. Both Dan and Joel stayed on for a few years.

Carl got frustrated with the bureaucracy and resigned shortly after I did. Laurie left the company to start a family around the time I left. The vast majority of the rest of the team stayed on for a few years, and a couple of folks are still with Jack Henry today. I enjoyed and greatly appreciate the contribution that each of them made to US Banking Alliance. For six years they were my family, and I miss them, our Friday lunches, and our company parties.

Even though things did not turn out anything like I expected, I am grateful that Jack Henry purchased my company. My life changed dramatically, and I continue to have new experiences as a result of the transaction.

Life Lessons from Mr. Lucky

Meet your obligations, no matter what.

Say what you mean – be honest and direct.

Remember you have total control of your life.

Learn new skills – always.

Find the good.

CHAPTER 23
Life is Short – Do It

Seven months after I retired, on May 31, 2008, Dawn and I drove our two elderly dogs, Rocky and Benny, to Sarasota, Florida to move into our new home. Dawn's dream was to live on the water, and we were fortunate that we had an opportunity to make it come true. We started our search in Clearwater, where Dawn had gone to high school. In barely an hour we decided there were too many strip malls and we were out of there. We spent a half-day in St. Petersburg, which seemed pretty nice. The next day we went to Sarasota and fell in love with it immediately, especially the waterfront. After a short search we found our dream house on the water. As an added bonus, we are only three hours from Florida Field, home of the University of Florida Fighting Gators.

Three days after we arrived, Melanie flew down from Atlanta after spending some time with friends. Dawn and I couldn't have been more excited to start the next phase of our lives. Melanie, thirteen at the time, did not share our enthusiasm. In fact, when we pulled up to our gorgeous new home she started crying hysterically, saying that her life was over, asking how we could possibly do this to her!

We recognized that moving during our daughter's teenage years wasn't ideal, and we didn't know anyone in Sarasota. The typical solution would have been to wait until Mel went off to college, but that was five years away. Even though we loved Atlanta and had lots of fabulous friends, in the previous eight years each of us had lost a parent and Dawn's brother had died tragically. As a result, we decided that life was full of uncertainties and this would be a good opportunity to move forward and live for today.

Sports Update

The relocation to Sarasota was a lucky one for our new favorite American League baseball team, the Tampa Bay Devil Rays. The team not only dropped Devil from their name and had their first winning record in their franchise's history, but they actually won the American League Championship five months after we arrived.

The college football season was even more memorable, as Tim Tebow and the Gators won their second college football national championship game in three years. And yours truly was able to go to Dolphin Stadium to attend the Gators' 24-14 Bowl Championship Series victory over Oklahoma.

And Then the Phone Rang

Ten months after I moved to Sarasota, Carl called to let me know that he and three other guys were starting a company to help banks with loan pricing. He couldn't imagine doing so without at least picking my brain, since I was the only one in the country who had ever done this.

We had a long, fascinating conversation about so many things. He told me that he didn't believe Jack Henry had done much to update the pricing software over the last two years; and he thought the need for good loan pricing software was as strong as when I had started my company. He pointed out that technology had changed dramatically and he could now build something far superior, given that he would be starting from scratch. He also reminded me that our two-year non-compete term had passed.

As excited as I was for him, the idea of competing against Jack Henry, including my former employees, initially made me uncomfortable. Carl was matter-of-fact, saying that Jack Henry had the opportunity to take our solution, which was best of class, and build a world-class solution. Two years later they should have been unstoppable. Instead, they had milked the relationship by doing the bare minimum for their clients, who were paying them an annual licensing fee.

Carl had looked at a lot of different business opportunities and kept coming back to the idea that this was the best. If he didn't do this, someone else would. The more we talked, the more comfortable I got with the Jack Henry issue and the more interested I was to be part of this opportunity. I was especially excited about the possibility of working with Carl again.

When I got off the phone, Dawn and I started talking about the business and me "going back to work." Most of my friends didn't think I would stay retired, even though Dawn and I completely believed I would. The opportunity to work with Carl again was appealing for two reasons. Just talking with Carl and hearing his perspective on things is always enlightening. Most significant, I greatly appreciated how instrumental he'd been in helping to dramatically increase the value of US Banking Alliance. The opportunity to help Carl in any way I could was paramount to me.

Early in May of 2009, Carl and I met with the other partners – Ken Garcia, Greg Upham, and Patrick Hurley – to discuss the startup of what would become PrecisionLender (PL). Carl had known Ken for many years, as they had worked together on a couple of deals. Ken had worked closely with Greg for a number of years and had known Patrick since college. At our first meeting we determined each of our roles with the company and how it would be funded.

Originally, the plan was for me to work at about a 10 percent level. Before long I was up to 50 percent, which quickly became 100 percent. To be clear, no one expected me to do this but there was work to be done. I can't imagine doing anything at less than full speed, so this actually should not have been such a surprise to me. I enjoyed working on this initiative, and my partners were all hard-working and totally committed to the success of the company.

Even though Carl was the business leader and he had the largest ownership position, I was originally named the CEO and Chairman, as I was the only one known to the community banking world. Operationally we treated each other as equals, and no one was the least bit concerned with titles. We were all focused on doing what was best for the business.

After about four years, I recognized that I was creating undue stress for myself. I had become involved with the Sarasota Y Foundation, where my role had also increased dramatically, and I realized that my passion for the day-to-day work involved in building PrecisionLender to be a world-class solution provider had decreased. Both organizations had extremely important missions, but the opportunity to help less fortunate children and families felt far more compelling at this stage of my life. I informed my partners that I wanted to work my way back to a lesser role in the company, and they were completely supportive. I am now only involved with PL as an investor and member of the board of directors.

As a co-founder, I could not be more proud of how successful Precision-Lender has become and its tremendous potential. When we started ten years ago, we created and offered the most comprehensive and easy-to-use loan pricing software in the industry. Our first client was a small community bank in Plaquemine, Louisiana, with assets of around $200 million.

How cool is it that our little company was Microsoft's first client to completely operate in the cloud? In fact two years later, when PL barely had twenty clients, Carl was asked to be on Microsoft's Azure advisory board related to Cloud computing.

Today we have offices on three continents, and some of the largest banks in the world are our clients. Our use of automated intelligence (AI) almost immediately captures the larger banks' attention. Andi, our intelligent virtual analyst, augments the relationship manager's strengths with powerful data and specific recommendations to facilitate a positive relationship between the bank and its customers.

Lots of people are worried about the impact of AI on our society and certainly there are likely to be abuses, as there have been with other technological advances. That said, AI will solve some of society's greatest challenges, such as curing cancer, enhancing education, and reducing our energy needs and dramatically change our lives.

I'm also very proud that the management team has focused on creating a great corporate culture. PrecisionLender has been recognized as a top place to work each of the last four years by the *Charlotte Business Journal*.

Life Lessons from Mr. Lucky

Life is full of uncertainties – live for today.

Embrace change; it's the only thing that is constant.

New opportunities are everywhere.

CHAPTER 24

What the Heck am I Doing in a Yoga Class?

I am eternally grateful that yoga is now a significant part of my life. We all have many so-called life-changing experiences, and yoga is definitely one of mine. Traveling the country on business for twenty-five years gave me a chance to see a lot of places and meet a lot of wonderful people; but travel is not the easiest thing on your body. Let's just say I wasn't the most flexible person in the room the day I showed up for my first class eleven years ago.

I'm not sure how or why I ended up in that first class. Dawn had become a certified yoga instructor right around the time I started my company and had been doing yoga for many years before that. Now that I've experienced how life-changing it is, I asked her why she never told me about yoga when I so desperately needed it. She laughed and said that it was right there in front of me the whole time.

I guess it's the same for many of my guy friends now. They tell me that they would like to try yoga but they aren't flexible enough. News flash: you probably aren't going to be any more flexible next year. And these are some pretty smart guys. The other thing these smart guys haven't figured out is that there are a lot more women in the typical yoga class than there are men.

I'm not sure it's the proper thing to say, but in the interest of getting more men into the studio, which would make the world a better place, I am going to point out that the women don't wear a whole lot to the classes. As I said, I may not be the smartest guy but I'm not blind or stupid either.

Finding a good studio and the right teacher is essential. A few months after we moved to Sarasota, I started going to classes at Prana Yoga, and then I quickly decided to take some private lessons with the studio owner, Regina. She is an amazing person, and her years as a cardiac nurse and yogi have made her extremely knowledgeable about the human body. Regina has the patience of a saint, a huge heart, and she strongly encourages her students to go beyond the limits they set for themselves.

I had been doing yoga for about a year, meaning I was a beginner at best, when Regina held her first teacher training program: a two-hundred-hour Hatha Yoga teacher training. I say, with much gratitude, that she practically forced me to join the program with two other men and twelve women.

Teacher Training

Teacher training was one of the best experiences of my life. When I started, Regina would prop me up on two or three blankets so I could sit with my legs crossed in "easy pose" somewhat comfortably, for two or three minutes at a time. Another challenging pose was *virasana*, where you are kneeling while seated on a block. Regina told me to do both poses daily. The purpose of this was to help open my hips, which holds the key to opening up the rest of the body. I did these two things religiously, mostly when I watched TV, and although the progress seemed slow, I can now sit through almost any show in either position. This has been so impactful for me that I take a yoga block, instead of a chair, to outdoor music concerts or festivals.

Most people think of yoga as something that helps with flexibility, and it certainly does, but yoga also builds core strength. I can't quite do a handstand in the middle of the room, but pressing your own weight with just a little balancing help from the wall will build some muscles. Being able to do a headstand at age fifty is very empowering as well.

As significant as the physical strength and flexibility were, the group discussions and reading about the emotional body were more important. The yoga classes, especially the teacher training, allowed me to slow down and presented an opportunity to be with my emotions. For the most part, I'm proud of who I am and how I have carried myself in life, but this process was eye-opening and not always easy.

As I mentioned, I have run through life at a fast pace, almost always "doing" and rarely "feeling," particularly during the difficult times, such as when our house burned down and when my father had cancer. I also recognize that I was not as aware of, or considerate of, how my actions impacted Dawn, Melanie, the rest of my family, my coworkers, and friends. I wasn't as understanding of what was happening in their lives as I would like to have been either. In addition to helping me become conscious of these things, yoga has also helped me recognize that beating myself up for my past mistakes doesn't benefit me or anyone else.

There are many insightful books, like Eckhart Tolle's *The Power of Now*, that I would never have read before I started doing yoga because I thought they were too "touchy-feely" or "out there." I took pride in the fact that I was always on and that my brain was always analyzing something, certainly never resting. Why I never appreciated something so obvious as your brain needing a little rest is both comical and sad, in equal parts.

As Tolle explains and yoga teaches, we can't do anything about the past, and the future is just a figment of our imagination. We need to be present, to live and appreciate the moment. My mother, one of the world's greatest worriers, shared that almost nothing that she worried about has actually happened. This is a lesson I hope I will learn soon.

Breathing and Practice

One of the most crucial aspects of yoga that we studied in detail in the teacher training was the power of our breath. I know it probably sounds crazy when I point out that we breathe all day long, from the moment we are born until the last second of our lives, and yet most of us really don't know how to breathe. I certainly didn't. Unless you were taught to sing or play a musical instrument, probably no one has ever talked with you about breathing except to suggest you take a couple of deep breaths before you are about to face a stressful situation.

In addition to basically learning how to breathe, we learned an endless number of simple techniques, including ones for relaxing, becoming more energized, better digestion, to cool off, to think more clearly, to lose weight, and for better overall health. Here is a simple one to try when you are having a tough time sleeping or are in a stressful situation. Inhale slowly for a count of four and exhale slowly for a count of six or eight (if possible). Continue for as long as necessary.

I didn't take teacher training with the goal of teaching. I just loved practicing yoga, and I practice every day, often more than once. If you're wondering about the reference to "practicing" rather than "doing" yoga, this is merely a reminder that we're on a never-ending journey that changes daily; this means that some days a pose will be easier than on others, and the more we advance, the more opportunity there is for further advancement. When you actually stop and think about this statement you realize that it applies equally well to life's always-changing journey.

Get Your Freak On

Yoga has helped me expand my horizons and open myself up to new things, and what's incredibly exciting is that there is always so much more. For example, Dawn switched from doing hatha yoga to kundalini yoga eight years ago and loves it. Kundalini is said to be the yoga of awareness brought from India by Yogi Bhajan to California in the late sixties. Among his many objectives, he wanted to show the hippies that by using a series of postures, hand positions, mantras, and breathing practices, they could experience a sense of euphoria without drugs.

Kundalini is a science-based technology that balances the glandular system, strengthens the nervous system, expands lung capacity, and purifies the blood. Each kriya, a series of exercises ranging from three minutes long to hours, has a different effect, but each kriya – and there are thousands – works on all levels of physical, mental, and spiritual well-being.

About two years ago Dawn started teaching a kundalini class once a week. Around that time, I said I would go with her to a class, not necessarily one she was teaching, to give it a try. Just as she never pushed me toward yoga years ago, she wasn't asking me when I would finally try a class. So for about six months, I always had some bogus reason why it wasn't a good time for her "freak yoga," even though I was going to a yoga class several times a week and practicing daily.

One Tuesday at about 9:40 I received a text from Regina saying that she couldn't make our standard 10:00 private training session. I knew Dawn was teaching a kundalini class in our home in twenty minutes. I guess the stars had finally aligned, so I walked upstairs and put my mat down for my first class. It was very different from any yoga class I had ever taken but I thoroughly enjoyed it.

Strangely enough, the next day I went to my usual yoga class that Regina normally taught, and there was a substitute teacher. As people were gathering for class, this teacher told us she had just graduated from kundalini teacher training. Something happened that hadn't ever occurred before; the class took a vote and decided to have her teach a kundalini class instead of the scheduled hatha yoga class. So there I was, after avoiding kundalini for six months, taking my second class in two days, which I also enjoyed.

Within a week I switched from hatha to kundalini, and I have only taken a handful of hatha classes in the last two years. Each kundalini class is different, based on the teacher and the kriya being taught. The classes are similar in that they all begin by tuning in and end with the class singing a song called "Long Time Sun." I don't want to scare you off kundalini yoga by saying it's different, a little weird, and somewhat freaky, but I think that's a fair description. I also think it's amazing, challenging, and totally wonderful.

I truly believe that everyone would benefit from it, but yoga, including kundalini yoga, isn't for everyone. That said, my greatest hope is that each person who reads this book will try three classes of kundalini yoga. Just to give you a little taste, I encourage you to go online and listen to Snatam Kaur sing "Long Time Sun." In three minutes and fifty-seven seconds, I hope her soothing and melodic voice will help you feel calmer and more relaxed, and make it easier to handle whatever life throws at you.

Every day I am more aware and appreciative of the impact kundalini yoga is having on me. I am calmer and more energized when I leave class and believe I'm stronger and more flexible as well. I have the most fabulous teacher, my wife. Last May Dawn finished her formal kundalini teacher training, and she is now teaching two classes a week, with all the class proceeds going to Snatam Kaur's summer kundalini camp for kids.

Dawn reads, practices, and studies anything and everything about kundalini yoga on a daily basis. Her students feel the loving energy she brings to the class and are so appreciative that they have the opportunity to practice with her in the simple but lovely studio that she created in our home. After each class I am more in awe of the joy and radiance that Dawn shares with us. It is a joy to see my wife so happy and making such a difference in the lives of so many.

And I haven't even mentioned what a terrific gong player she is. At the end of each class she plays the gong for about ten minutes, which provides a sound therapy that is calming, energizing, and healing. I almost always fall asleep during this deep relaxation.

I was fortunate to tag along and participate in some of Dawn's teacher training classes, as well as meet many of the students and all of her teachers. As much as I enjoy a typical class, the energy in a training class with forty or fifty people is even more powerful. The last week of her teacher training was held in Majorca, a beautiful island off the coast of Spain. The class did a couple of spiritual retreats to remote, magical places, and I was able to connect with these awesome people. I know this may sound kooky, but I believe the world would be a kind, gentle, loving, and peaceful place if everyone regularly practiced yoga.

I Can Dance and Maybe Even Sing

An embarrassing aside I would like to share relates to singing and dancing. Twenty-nine years ago, when I saw our wedding video, I was shocked to find out that I was a horrible dancer. One day a couple of years ago my sweet wife blurted out, "When did you learn to dance?" I have no illusions about my abilities, but I believe my dancing partially reflects a looser body from the yoga and other bodywork I am doing. And Dawn's comment sure made me happy because dancing is such fun.

Another enjoyable aspect of kundalini is that classes sometimes include a few minutes of chanting, in addition to the two chants at the beginning and the song at the end of class. I am not sure of the most accurate way to describe my singing career, but in the sixth or seventh grade I wanted to learn to play drums. The only "tryout" consisted of the music teacher asking us to sing. She immediately squashed my musical career big time, and I have rested my vocal cords ever since.

The vast majority of a kundalini class is done with your eyes closed so that you go inside and have your own experience. You also don't compare yourself to others and aren't distracted by anyone. This may sound silly, but it feels a little safer to sing when everyone's eyes are closed. I started chanting at a little more than a whisper two years ago, and I now let my voice be heard. Much to my shock, a few people have told me that I have a nice singing voice. I still don't walk around the house singing joyously like my wife does, but maybe that will happen soon. Or perhaps I'll be a singer in a rock 'n' roll band in my next life – or my dream tonight!

Life Lessons from Mr. Lucky

Yoga can change your life.

The best time to try it is now.

Find a great teacher.

Your brain needs to rest.

Learn to breathe.

Just try three classes.

CHAPTER 25

Sarasota is an Amazing Place

arasota, Florida is an exceptional place to live, with the most beautiful beaches in the world (Siesta Key Beach has been rated the best more than once), excellent arts and theater, and a surprisingly vibrant local music scene (especially if you are an Allman Brothers fan). It is home to two highly ranked colleges (Ringling College of Art and Design and New College of Florida) and is blessed with a generous philanthropic community.

Philanthropy 101

The opportunity to help people, animals, and any and every cause under the sun can be super fun and highly rewarding. Dawn and I were excited to be at the giving-back stage of our lives, although my time was limited while I was starting the new venture with PrecisionLender. As in all aspects of life, however, we would learn some brutal lessons; in this case, they were about the charity world.

Dawn's new best friend, Debbie Dannheisser, and Debbie's husband Dan were heavily involved in local charities, in particular the Sarasota YMCA.

Dawn followed her friend's lead and became a Y Angel – a group of fabulous women who gave a lot of time and money to the Y.

Over time, I learned that the Y was not just another swim and gym facility, but rather an organization devoted to changing the lives of many needy children and families. I was shocked when I heard that the city I had come to love had over 1,000 homeless students. The Sarasota Y helps these students get to school and have something to eat before they arrive. Their Triad School helps kids who are expelled from other schools get a high school degree. The youth shelter provides a safe place and temporary home for runaway, homeless, and troubled youth. The Y-Achievers was mentoring hundreds of students. The Y is also responsible for the Safe Children Coalition program, which is a large foster-care program. I could go on and on about the Y programs. Suffice it to say, I learned that the Y is much more than a place to work out.

Dawn quickly stepped up and co-chaired two galas for the Y. Co-chairing the gala was an endless amount of work, but provided a fantastic opportunity to meet caring people and help those less fortunate in the community.

In the beginning I was primarily an observer, going to the events, supporting my wife who was doing the hard work, and occasionally hosting a charity event at our house. Hosting an event at your house typically involves much less work and is way more fun. I was basically responsible for two things: donating our favorite wines and arranging for amazing musicians to play. There aren't many things more fantastic than having a band play in your living room, especially at the end of the night when most of the people have left, and the band wants to keep playing. For the most fun, keep the band well hydrated!

One of Life's Biggest Joys

Participating in the Y Mentor Program took my involvement in the Y to the next level and gave me the most satisfaction. In roughly an hour a week, two people can make a meaningful connection that changes both of their lives. As the mentor, I was able to share my life skills and experiences in a completely new way.

My first two mentoring relationships were challenging at best. Joe was a reasonably bright senior in high school who didn't apply himself and was somewhat socially awkward. He came from a relatively typical middle-class family, but didn't have a good relationship with his parents. His favorite activity was gaming, which I didn't know much about, and we never connected in a consequential way.

In early December 2012 I met my next student, Mike, a ninth grader. He looked like a guy who could play middle linebacker for the Gators. Two things made it unlikely that he would ever set foot on Florida Field, though. First, he was a Florida State Seminole fan. I wasn't going to let that stop me from trying to recruit the kid. The bigger, more challenging issue was his 0.9 grade point average, which precluded him from even playing on the Sarasota High School ninth grade football team.

For a period of time I thought I could be the guy to turn Mike around. He was a nice kid, but he had a little attitude when it came to his teachers, who he always thought were picking on him. I did everything I could think of to motivate him; however, most of the time he just BSed me and didn't follow through on what he committed to doing. At one point I was even able to get his mother to give me the code to the school assignment/grade tracking software so I could monitor what was really happening.

Mike wanted to be on the football team, so I used this and my knowledge of football recruiting to try to get him to focus in class and do his schoolwork. He would often say that he didn't feel like paying attention or studying that day. I asked him how often he had told his coaches that he didn't feel like practicing or doing a drill, and what they would say if he told them he was a little tired that day. He always acted as though he got the message, but nothing changed. His mother and grandmother believed that doing well in school was critical, and the school also worked hard to help Mike. I gave it my best, but at the end of the school year he still had a 0.9 grade point average.

In the fall, when the mentor program started back up, I spoke to the program coordinator and then the vice principal of the high school about continuing to mentor Mike. I did not want to give up on him. I also didn't want to waste my time with someone who didn't appear to benefit from the relationship. When Mike told the vice principal that he was not interested in having a mentor, I was relieved. I'm sure I would have stuck with him if he'd asked for another chance, but it probably would have been an exercise in frustration and might have soured me on mentoring.

I had a lengthy conversation about the first two guys with the awesome woman who headed the mentor program, Kathy Chamberlain. Both of us agreed that I would be better off mentoring someone more academically ambitious. She called me the next week and said she had the perfect situation for me. I met Coy Carter shortly thereafter, and she was so right. Both of our lives have been changed forever.

The mentoring process had started a little rough for me, but once I got the students with whom I clicked, it became one of the great joys of my life. I met Coy about six years ago, when he was finishing his senior year in high school. He was part of the Class program that the Y created with the State of Florida for approximately ten homeless students. The program assisted them with reduced-cost housing as long as they were full-time students and worked at least thirty hours a week. Not easy criteria by any means, especially since they had to secure the housing on their own and maintain the apartment as well. This wasn't standard dorm living on campus with a meal plan, etc. These students had to do everything themselves.

About a year later I started mentoring Jeron Thomas when he also entered the Class program. Neither he nor Coy initially wanted a mentor, but thankfully this was a program requirement. Both of them are wonderful individuals who were raised by their moms and lacked a good male role model.

For about six years I have been getting together each week with Coy and have been doing the same with Jeron for almost five years. We meet for coffee or lunch and talk about whatever is going on in their lives. In the beginning we would start out talking about sports or something impersonal to break the ice and then get into school, work, healthy eating, family, saving money, and even the scary subject of relationships.

Just Be There for Someone

After those first few months of gaining their trust, both Coy and Jeron now sit down and just start talking. As a mentor, one never knows what is going to come up in each meeting. Sometimes I am exposed to issues and challenges that I have virtually no knowledge about, or experience with, in my own life. This has helped me become a better listener, and I believe that I have much greater empathy for others. I am in awe of their motivation and determination to overcome so many obstacles. Knowing them has also helped me feel more optimistic about the future.

In the beginning of these relationships, one of the most important things was to just show up each week. If I was traveling, I would check in with a text or send them a thoughtful quote. I deeply care about both young men, and they know it. They have each told me that no one has ever consistently been there for them the way I have.

Be Part of the Solution

Being a mentor is a combination of being a friend, coach, parent, and teacher. Yet it's so different than being a parent; my daughter only wants to hear what

I have to say half the time. Perhaps they have me fooled, but I think the guys are actually interested in what I have to say.

Being a mentor is also very different than being a donor. As a donor, I hope that the money I give creates value, but I typically don't get to truly see or feel the impact. One of the benefits of being a mentor is getting to see and hear every week what has happened in the mentee's life. Although the impact of my meetings was not apparent immediately, and the relationships were not always easy, I believed I was making a difference in their lives and knew that they were making a difference in mine.

In business I learned that to be successful you need to create value for others. The more effectively you can communicate this, the more successful you will be. That part of my life is mostly over, and I am happy to say that what I'm doing now is even better. The last few years I have been focused on creating value for others. The difference – the big difference now – is that I have no goal other than truly helping others. I encourage everybody to be a mentor. Giving money to charity is highly impactful, but being there and being part of someone's life is extremely rewarding.

Coy just graduated from the University of South Florida (USF) with his MBA and has been a licensed real estate agent for over two years. He recently bought a house, and during his last semester of grad school he not only passed his real estate brokerage exam, he took on a second job. His goal was to make two payments a month on his mortgage instead of one in order to quickly eliminate paying private mortgage insurance. Wow, that is impressive! Coy almost always has a big smile on his face and has started working on healing the heavy things from his past.

Jeron is a senior at USF. While I'm curious to see what he ends up doing when he graduates, I have no worries about him being successful in life. He is an inspiring young man – a full-time student who also works thirty-plus hours a week serving both ends of the social spectrum, at the Ritz-Carlton and at Everyday Blessings, a foster care home. Jeron is hard-working, responsible, intelligent, thoughtful, kind, caring, and sensitive. He cares as much about how others are being treated as he does about how he is treated. He is more in touch with himself and comfortable talking about relationships than almost all of the men I know who are thirty and forty years older than he is.

Jeron spoke at a luncheon and shared something powerful with the group. He said that there was a point recently where he had heard me say how amazing he was enough times that he finally believed in himself. Those words were very gratifying to me. There is so much satisfaction and joy in watching someone else improve their life and achieve success.

Life Lessons from Mr. Lucky

The opportunity to help people is unlimited.

The world of charity presents many great opportunities.

Mentoring allows you to see the impact you are having.

Be part of the solution.

CHAPTER 26

The More You Give, the More You Get

H opefully you learned a long time ago what I learned over the last several years: the more you give, the more you get. Before moving to Sarasota I was too busy to care about much more than my family, my business, and my friends. I had no time or concern for the many heartbreaking things going on, not just in the world, but also right in my backyard.

Going to charity events in Sarasota and hearing stories from recipients of their work woke me up. Now I am proud to be part of the solution, not just by writing a check but also by spending a lot of my time trying to be of help to others. While there are many awesome organizations in the area, the Sarasota Y Foundation resonated with me the most and became a very important part of my life.

Back to Work

The Foundation's chairman and president invited me to lunch to talk about joining their board. Everything seemed pretty straightforward, but this would be my first board role for a charity. Given my experience with Jack Henry & Associates, I was concerned about whether the Foundation operated in a slow-moving, bureaucratic way. The chairman assured me that it did not. He told me that this wasn't a lifetime appointment, and if I wasn't happy I could resign and there would be no hard feelings. This was enough to convince me to take things to the next level, and I agreed to join the board.

Once I was approved, I got involved in a big way. The first year I was put on the Investment Committee. Year two I also chaired a startup committee to help create a young philanthropists' group and I agreed to co-chair the annual gala. The following year I went all in. In addition to co-chairing the gala again, I got talked into becoming the chairman of the Y Foundation. What I was thinking?

I can assure you that I wasn't sitting around bored. On the contrary, I was enjoying life after years of working way too hard. The reason for my commitment to the Y was simple. Over the last few years, I had learned that our wonderful city of Sarasota has many challenges. The Y was at the forefront of making a difference in so many ways, and I absolutely wanted to be part of the solution.

A Peek Behind the Curtain

No sooner had I become board chairman of the Foundation than I found out how challenged the relationship was between the Y CEO and the Y Foundation president, Jennifer Grondahl. After gathering a little information, I met with the chairman of the Y board to discuss a few things. He quickly shared information with me that was clearly untrue.

As I've said, honesty and integrity are critical to me in all aspects of life. I should have known that day that I was in for the shock of my life.

I need to quickly digress to explain the structure of the Sarasota Y. There is an operating entity that is responsible for all of the Y's programs and social services. I will refer to them and their board of directors as the Y. The Y

Foundation, of which I was chairman, was a separate organization, and was responsible for all the fundraising and the endowment.

I'll spare you most of the details of what occurred over the next ten months leading up to our big gala and the ensuing blowup between the two organizations, except for some background information. We made three separate, lengthy attempts to work through a couple of basic issues that involved considerable time, monetary expense, and emotional energy. The basic issues were that the Y believed there was no real need for the Foundation and wanted total control over how the operation was run and how the money we raised was spent. The Foundation believed that the Y was not run efficiently.

In hindsight, the best or worst thing that happened was the Y folks suggested that one way to create more continuity between the two organizations was for both board chairmen to attend each other's board meetings. Additionally, we would each have representation at the respective finance committee meetings. This would allow both groups to learn about, and appreciate, the challenges and opportunities of the other.

I attended almost all of their board and finance committee meetings and sent a representative for the couple that I couldn't make. I didn't just go to the meetings; I asked questions, gave my opinion, and made suggestions.

Our Money Wasn't Really Supporting the Cause

As board chairman and co-chair of the gala, I was giving money and asking my friends and others in the community to give to this life-changing organization because I believed that it helped many less-fortunate families and children. After attending a few of these meetings, I learned that almost all of the funding for these services was provided by government agencies. The money from our donors was mostly supporting an inefficiently operated swim and gym program, including its youth swim team.

Dawn and I, as well as the Foundation board, all of whom gave a significant amount of money, were not happy about how our money was being used. I believed that our friends would have minimal, if any, interest in continuing to give money to support the organization if we didn't address these issues. The Y board gave an endless number of unsatisfactory reasons for their deteriorating operational results and was not focused on addressing these issues. Instead, they pointed fingers at the Foundation's fundraising. Oddly enough, the majority of Y board members donated very little money and didn't help with the fundraising.

The Big Night

On Saturday May 7th, the Foundation hosted its most successful Going for the Gold Gala, which netted over $600,000. This capped off the organization's best fundraising year ever. Ironically, at the after-party the Y CEO was alleged to have performed a hat trick, making sexist, racist, and homophobic comments to a group of attendees that included employees from both groups, their friends, and a Y board member. The incident also involved a claim of employee harassment.

Despite the Foundation's insistence, the Y board was unwilling to perform a proper investigation and address the allegations. The CEO of a publicly traded company and an attorney both resigned from the Y board, knowing they could not be part of an organization that failed to govern itself appropriately.

As the Foundation's board chair, I met with and talked to members of both boards and other concerned individuals in the community, hoping to find a solution to the twin problems of governance and financial discipline. The first problem should have been a no-brainer. The #MeToo movement has shown that organizations have no choice but to deal with sexual harassment issues, no matter who the individual is; and like most of those accused of harassment, the Y CEO was not the proverbial Boy Scout. The Y board remained adamant that nothing more than a warning was necessary.

Had the personnel issue been addressed in a timely and appropriate manner, perhaps the financial issues could have been resolved. The facts were relatively straightforward. Both the Y and the Foundation were not operationally efficient. The Y had worked for years to fix its financial problems. In fairness, from its weakest point, there was improvement. However, there was no improvement in 2016 and none was even budgeted for in 2017. In the Y's strategic planning meeting in late May, the facilitator, a senior person from Y USA, stated that funding depreciation and reserves are considered "best practices." The Y did not have either a short-term or a long-term plan to fund depreciation and reserves. As Foundation chairman, I knew this crucial subject had never even been discussed with the Y's Board.

The Foundation had faced the same difficult economic environment, yet in the three years since it had hired Jennifer as president, it doubled the amount of funds raised, with less than a 10 percent increase in expenses. While there was definitely more work to be done, she had done an excellent job and the momentum was clearly moving in the right direction.

Two Different Approaches

A quick example will hopefully illustrate the totally different mindsets of the two organizations. Once the Y recognized that the Foundation was done funding its deficit spending, their first action was to terminate the person in charge of the mentor program. This saved roughly $50,000 from a $39 million budget at the expense of approximately five hundred students. Three years prior, when the Y wanted to cut this unbelievably valuable program, Jennifer made one phone call and a generous Foundation board member committed to fund the entire $50,000.

The last two months of the Foundation's existence were even more physically and emotionally exhausting, as we tried desperately to strike a deal with the Y. The Foundation board, especially the Executive Committee, worked endlessly to find a solution. This wasn't a corporate board fighting for survival; these were volunteers who absolutely believed in the Y's mission to help the many less-fortunate families and individuals in our community. No matter what we said or did, or who we brought to the table to help, we were unable to make progress.

One Last Try

Our final effort to save the organization was to suggest a merger between the Y board and the Foundation board. Unfortunately, emotions and egos got in the way. The Y felt our merger proposal was a hostile takeover, as the Foundation insisted on greater representation on the board and the key executive committee positions. The Foundation believed there was no other way, as the Y had clearly lacked moral character, good governance practices, and was not fiscally responsible. There was a lot of work to be done and we didn't want to end up just banging our heads against the wall. On a sad day late in September, our board voted unanimously to shut down our fundraising efforts. I wish I could say that ended this part of the journey but actually another seven months of pain followed during the winding-down phase, as we did our best to protect donor funds.

Find the Good

My year as board chair was unbelievably challenging as we navigated between huge, petty potholes and tremendous fundraising success. I felt terrible for Jennifer. She had done an outstanding job as president, bringing in new major donors and doubling contributions, all while dealing with an endless number of obstacles created by the Y CEO and many on his board.

I'm not sure which of us was raked over the coals more by the Y board, her or me, but we were determined to help the families and especially the kids. Jennifer and her committed team stuck together for the cause and each other, in spite of everything.

I spent months on the firing line, working as a volunteer for something I believed in. I took calls and participated in meetings at the worst conceivable times of the day, including many while I was on vacation, because I wanted to be part of the solution. In hindsight, I would have done some things differently, but only in small ways.

I am proud to have made the effort without sacrificing my principles. In the end, sometimes you just have to let go and trust the universe. Hopefully new leadership at the Y will address the fundamental problems of the business. I won't root against them, as there are too many people in our community who need their services. Given how generous our community is, I'm sure that if the worst happens, people and other charitable organizations will step in to minimize the disruption.

I will be forever grateful to the Y's mentor program for introducing Coy and Jeron to me. They have taught me so much and made me a kinder, gentler, more empathetic person. Our relationships continue to grow. The guys come over to our house or we go to see a motivational speaker or a ballgame. When my daughter is in town, we invite them over or do something fun as a group, and the guys get together fairly regularly on their own, which makes me extremely happy. I see no reason why we won't all be a significant part of each other's lives forever.

I am also thankful for the many other friends that resulted from my involvement with the Y. In addition, I'm happy to report that a few of the Foundation board members started an organization called Faces of Accomplishment that mentors students and provides college scholarships.

Life Lessons from Mr. Lucky

Charities have problems too.

Nothing is more important than honesty and integrity.

Emotions and egos can be hard to overcome.

Search for the silver lining.

CHAPTER 27
Nurturing Dads Program

Children First, with its terrific inspirational CEO, Philip Tavill, is a phenomenal organization in Sarasota that provides services to more than six hundred vulnerable children from birth to age five and their families. Their Head Start program is arguably the best in the country. They also offer a Nurturing Dads program, which gives new dads an opportunity to get together weekly to talk about being a father. Melanie was a junior in high school when I was asked to observe the class with the possibility of becoming a facilitator.

From my perspective, the most meaningful aspect of the class involved an exercise in which we created a vision statement: "The father I choose to be." To start the exercise, we each wrote down the characteristics and qualities of our father's parenting style, with an emphasis on how he made us feel. We then indicated which of these traits we wanted to keep and enhance; which we wanted to avoid (many at all costs); and whatever else we wanted to add.

This exercise was intensely thought-provoking, and I found it very emotional to see and hear so many of the dads share their heartbreaking stories of having been neglected and abused. I think back on my childhood much more favorably. However, I know that my dad's decision to move to

Florida when I was fourteen was unquestionably horrendous and had a big impact on my high school years.

I would like to share the Nurturing Dad's flyer with ten tips for being a great dad:

1. Show up – Be there for your children.
2. Support and respect your children's mother.
3. Listen – Earn the right to be heard.
4. Discipline with love.
5. Be a role model – Teach by example.
6. Know and be known to the people in your children's world.
7. Play with your children and read to your children.
8. Show affection – Let them know you love them.
9. Help out – Take an active role (homework, housework, etc.).
10. Keep a sense of humor.

This list and the class are good examples of how powerful a simple, common-sense approach can be. When you think about society's many challenges, the family structure is certainly near the top of the list, as far too many kids are raised by a single parent. Even in the best of circumstances, most parents, particularly men, have little or no preparation for what is arguably their most meaningful job.

A few of the fathers in this class were there because the court ordered them to attend. However, I experienced firsthand the value of the Nurturing Dads program, and I absolutely encourage all dads to take part in a program like this. We had thoughtful conversations and candidly shared our experiences with one another. We all left the class better prepared to love and support our children and their mother. Those fathers who were no longer in relationships with the mother were given guidance as well.

Item number three reminds me of a simple saying that originated in 55 AD: "You were born with two ears and one mouth for a reason, so that we can listen twice as much as we speak." Occasionally we will be in a group setting and someone will point out that I have been awfully quiet. Although it's tempting to respond that most people talk too much or that the conversation was really about nothing, I usually just try to smile. The truth is that silence is often golden.

Life Lessons from Mr. Lucky

There is no more important job than being a parent.

Listen twice as much as you speak.

Find out about the Nurturing Dads program.

Be the best parent you can be.

CHAPTER 28
Managing Your Finances is Essential

O ne of the things that Dawn and I are passionate about is helping deserving students afford a college education. During the process of writing this book, one of my friends and co-founders of PrecisionLender, Ken Garcia, recommended that I read *Rich Dad, Poor Dad,* an engaging book written by Robert T. Kiyosaki and Sharon L. Lechter in 1997. (There have been updated editions since.) While I didn't agree with some of the financial strategies in the book, the discussion about financial literacy definitely hit home.

I absolutely believe that the vast majority of both high school and college graduates have received little, if any, information or training about money management or how to be financially successful in life. I will go a step further and say that many adults are no more knowledgeable about this topic than recent graduates. There are many challenges within our country's education system but this glaring weakness is rarely mentioned.

Numerous studies indicate that over 50 percent of Americans have less than $500 of savings. While there are many outstanding books on personal finance, I would like to share some of the things I learned early in my career that helped to position me for financial success well before I had my own business.

Buying a House – the Millionaire Next Door

There are a lot of philosophies regarding buying a house. My fraternal grandparents recommended buying the biggest house possible. Dawn and I took the opposite route, which was recommended in a book that had a big impact on me, *The Millionaire Next Door*, written by Thomas J. Stanley and William D. Danko.

The major premise of the book is to live below one's means and accumulate wealth rather than spending most or all of your earnings. Our society is so focused on having the right stuff, now, whether or not we can afford it. Buying the biggest house you can creates a lot of financial stress, as you have more house to furnish, heat, and maintain. Also, the odds are your neighbors will have more "fun money" than you. This creates additional financial strain if you live in the type of neighborhood where people socialize with one another. Additionally, you have no money left for savings.

Dawn and I practiced what I am preaching with each of the houses we lived in, never stretching during the buying process. In 1999 we moved into a brand-new subdivision with thirty-nine houses. One of our next-door neighbors was a couple about ten years younger. They bought virtually the same home we did, except this was our fourth home and their first. I'm not making a judgment about their buying decision or situation, as they have a great family, have been successful professionally, and we are good friends. I would point out, however, that they didn't buy dining room furniture for four or five years.

Becoming Wealthy – Part I: How to Turn $3.29 a Day Into $671,474

You might think that the key to becoming wealthy is to make a lot of money, but perhaps even more significant is how much money you spend and when you start to save.

Let me share some mind-blowing numbers with you. If you save $100 a month starting at age twenty-three and earn eight percent a year in a 401(k) plan (the long-term average of the S&P 500 index over the past ninety years was 9.8%), you will have $335,737 in forty years. If you wait until you are forty-three to start saving, you will have to save $567 a month to end up with the same amount of money. In the first scenario you saved a total of $48,000 and in the second scenario you had to save $136,080.

I'm not just talking theory here, as I actually started saving when I received my first paycheck with the Federal Reserve, contributing six percent of my salary to their 401(k) plan. While I was fortunate to graduate college with no debt, I would like to remind you that I graduated with a starting salary that was at, or near, the bottom of my MBA class.

The absolute best investment vehicle is a 401(k) program. If your employer matches all of your contribution, like the Fed did mine, you are starting with a 100 percent return on your investment. This is one of the few real examples of free money, so at a minimum you need to contribute enough to get the company match.

Let's go back to my initial scenario where you start saving $100 a month at age twenty-three, you don't ever increase how much you save, and your company matches the contribution. If you earn 8 percent a year, your $48,000 will turn into $671,474 in forty years. If that's not a holy smokes piece of information, I don't know what is!

Having said all that, the reality is that most Americans are living paycheck to paycheck, and few have anywhere near $671,474. Given how crucial this is, I'm going to say it again with a little different spin. This strategy basically turns $3.29 a day ($100 a month) into well over a half-million dollars!

A way to build your savings even more is to increase the amount you save each time you get a raise. If you are not able to do this, you're probably not living within your means. Let me be more direct: You're spending too much money.

Becoming Wealthy – Part 2

The other key factor to accumulating wealth is obviously controlling how much you spend. In this instant gratification society, a lot of people pay for things on credit. I'm not going to tell you not to do this; I'm just going to share a couple of numbers with you.

Let's say you pay $3,000 for your vacation or that "have to have" thing that you buy with a credit card that charges 15 percent (just below the national average), and you only pay the minimum amount (as charged by nine of the top ten credit card issuers). You will end up paying this debt off in seventeen years and ten months at a total cost of $6,229. In other words, you will pay more than double what you initially spent, and by the time you have paid off your purchase you probably won't even remember what you bought.

If you are just starting out or looking for some understandable, common-sense financial advice, grab a personal wealth management book by Suze Orman or Dave Ramsey. Their books and *The Millionaire Next Door* will set you up for life if you pay attention and follow their advice.

Our Approach

Dawn and I believed that setting aside money for a rainy day and investing for college and retirement were important. We also wanted to enjoy our life in the present. For most of our lives, this meant we had to make difficult financial choices. The first thing we did was pay off Dawn's credit cards. Once this was done, the only things we ever borrowed money to buy were a house and our cars. We did charge a lot of things on our credit cards to get mileage credits; however, we paid them off in full each month, always.

We bought our cars with a similar strategy as we did our homes, believing that this was a good way to save a lot of money and leave us with more fun money. In fact, I did not purchase a brand new vehicle for myself until I sold my business. Instead I purchased cars that were two or three years old and still had a manufacturer's warranty. In full disclosure, I did buy a couple of new cars for Dawn, but that wasn't until the business was doing well and we were in our forties.

One of the perks from my career was all the frequent flyer mileage and hotel points I earned, which allowed us to take many enjoyable vacations without spending a lot of money. We loved these trips, but we also wanted to enjoy ourselves the other fifty weeks of the year. Most people have to make choices, and we did as well. Our philosophy was to spend money on experiences rather than stuff.

Your Body is a Temple

Financial health is important but without our physical well-being, almost nothing matters. One of the positive things that came out of our infertility experience was a better understanding of the impact of what we put into our body. I am lucky because this is something my wife is interested in, so for the most part, I can just follow her lead or take her advice. Dawn became very knowledgeable about nutrition, medicine, vaccines, etc., including the products we place on our body and use in our house.

We eat a very healthy diet (she eats incredibly healthily), including as much organic food as possible. I have found that a lighter, more nutritious diet gives me more energy, and I believe this will mean better long-term health. While this is admittedly more costly, life is about choices, and I think that there is probably nothing more consequential than taking care of yourself and your loved ones. Assuming that money is an issue, at a minimum I recommend finding out which foods have the highest level of pesticides and buying organic instead. Here is a quick top ten list: apples, baby food, strawberries and blueberries, peaches and nectarines, celery, peanut butter, potatoes, milk, greens, and tomatoes. The Internet is obviously a good place for additional information.

I want to mention one of the most significant ways I improved my health. I completely stopped drinking soda and started drinking water all day long. I figured that anything that can be used to clean battery acid can't be very healthy. Not only is water calorie-free, it will help improve most of your bodily functions. As a side note, diet soda is probably even less healthy than regular soda.

I never smoked cigarettes and I was going to try not to mention them, but I can't help myself. I understand that if you smoke them, you are addicted and you have little control; however, nothing would help you more physically, mentally, and financially than to quit. At a pack a day, you would save at least $2,500 a year. Over forty years that's $100,000. And if you invested just half of the savings, in forty years you would have about $350,000. You will be healthier almost instantly, look younger longer, your food will taste better, and best of all, you will feel an unbelievable sense of accomplishment.

Nicotine being a dangerous toxin, I would also avoid e-cigarettes or vaping devices. Even nicotine-free vaping liquids contain flavoring chemicals that have been shown to damage the lungs, contributing to chronic coughs, bronchitis, and other ailments.

Life Lessons from Mr. Lucky

Learn about personal finance.

Start saving as soon as possible.

Pay off your credit cards in full every month.

Treat your body as if it's the most important thing.

Improve your diet.

Eliminate or at least drink less soda.

Drink lots of water.

CHAPTER 29

An Inexpensive Lesson and an Expensive One

My dad was a stockbroker/financial advisor his entire career. One summer when I was twenty-one, he helped me get a job working on the floor of the American Stock Exchange. My job there was as a reporter, which meant I worked in the pit at a station that traded options on stocks listed on the NY Stock Exchange. My responsibility was to report each trade: list the price, volume, and product traded, as well as update the bid and ask on each option. As a summer intern, I typically worked a station that was expected to be slow.

One particular Friday, late in the summer, I was working right next to the station that included the options for Dr. Pepper. The volume picked up dramatically, as rumors were flying that Dr. Pepper was going to be acquired. On my break I went to a phone booth (as one did back then) and quickly called my dad to tell him what was going on.

He placed an order to buy five August 15 calls; four of them were for him and one was for me. I'm a little foggy on the details of this transaction, as it took place thirty-eight years ago. I believe each option cost about $500, and that's what I gave my dad for my share of the trade. If an agreement to purchase Dr. Pepper was executed before the options expired in two weeks, we would be big winners!

What I do remember clearly was that the rumors died down almost immediately. Dr. Pepper was not acquired, so our options expired *worthless*. While this was a good share of my summer savings and extremely disappointing at the time, I learned an invaluable lesson for $500. In all likelihood, if this trade had worked out my next options trades would have involved more money, quite possibly serious money. And at some point, I would likely have incurred significant losses.

For the most part, options trading is nothing more than gambling, and whether it's Las Vegas or the NFL, most people lose money gambling. I never purchased any options again, so I figure learning this lesson early in my career was another of the many lucky things that has happened to me.

How to Treat Money: CVS

I have never taken money for granted, as I've seen how it impacts us all. I'll share a little story about which I am equally embarrassed and proud. I recently received an email from CVS stating that I was among the top 2 percent of their customers in annual savings. I often go into the store with a 30 or 40 percent off coupon and five or ten dollars in "extra care dollars" that I've earned from buying extra soft Charmin toilet paper and other products at just the right time.

To put this in perspective, the CVS is across the street from the yoga studio, so I'm not going out of my way. The reality is I get a kick out of buying $32-worth of stuff for $13 and have always felt that by doing little things like this I would always have enough money to live comfortably. Maybe I'm a little superstitious, but why should I stop doing easy things like this because I no longer need the money?

Some people might consider this to be cheap or beneath them, which goes back to another aspect of money that I find interesting. Everybody has a different opinion about how to spend their money. Most of the time I am very generous; but there are some days I'm just not feeling it. Sometimes I will recognize this later and wonder what happened. Other times Dawn will point this out or ask why I wasn't more generous. Of course she is usually right. One thing that bothers me and makes me highly resistant is when I feel pressured to do something or people make an assumption about what I should do with my money.

I think we all have a tendency at times to count other people's money and to have opinions about how they should spend it. But we never know anyone else's real financial situation. Did they make a bad investment decision or a series of bad financial choices? Are they caring for family? Do they quietly give a lot of money to charity? No matter the answers, what right do we have to judge other people about this or anything, especially since we have incomplete information? Unfortunately that doesn't stop us, and I will admit I am guilty at times as well.

An Expensive Lesson

Lending money to my uncle has been one of the most frustrating, disappointing, and painful things I have ever experienced. He is thirteen years older than me and used to babysit me when I was a kid. Mom tells me they would have to hide most of her amazing chocolate chip cookies when he came over, or he would eat them all. He liked to joke that he would throw me up in the air and drop me. Like most jokes, I suspect that there was some truth to this. But both of these stories reflect his youthful exuberance, as well as his sometimes selfish or reckless nature.

Although we didn't see each other as much as I would have liked over the years because we lived in different parts of the country, I always looked forward to getting together with my uncle and catching up. We would talk about all aspects of life, and he would usually probe deeply into what was happening in mine. I would share more with him than I would with most people. When I considered changing careers in my early thirties, he was one of the people I called for advice.

All of that changed when my wife and I became his lender of last resort. Occasionally I blame Dawn for convincing me to help my uncle, but deep down I know that is not fair or accurate; there is no one to blame except myself. Lest you think badly of me for not wanting to help my uncle, I will point out that when my father was alive, he wouldn't lend money to his younger brother for his many mediocre business ventures. Although they weren't wild, crazy ventures, most of them turned out to be less successful than he hoped. This time he wanted to buy an International House of Pancakes (IHOP). When I told my mother that we had lent my uncle money she was highly skeptical.

So why did I lend him money, or should I say a *lot* of money? A *whole lot* of money. He is a master at using guilt to get what he wants, as he was a psychologist early in his career. When it suits him, everything is about family and of course families help one another. He harassed me for hours on end with his tales of woe, pressuring me to help him out. I would get off many of our phone calls sick to my stomach, feeling as if there was something wrong with me for not wanting to help out my uncle. Then we would do it all over a couple of days later. I was so tense after each call that my body would be in a knot.

In the end he wore me down, and we agreed to lend him the money he asked for. That's when the real problems began. He consistently let me down, failing to do what he said he would do. When he needed something, it was usually immediate. When I needed something from him – documentation or information – I got it on "island time." Speaking of time, it was a rare occurrence for his checks to arrive on the first of the month. Many other times, his check would bounce.

Each time this happened it meant another long call, trying to find out what was going on with his business. At best the discussions left me with the same knots in my stomach, frustrated and disappointed. I started believing "No good deed goes unpunished," which is contrary to my true belief system. This wasn't the way I would treat anyone, let alone a family member who was helping me out.

I remember one time I discovered around ten o'clock at night that his check had bounced. I called him immediately to see what was going on. He was very annoyed that I had inconvenienced him by not having waited until the morning to call him. Let me tell you, if the roles had been reversed and I was having troubles, I would have either asked for some advice, additional financial assistance, or at the least, given him a heads-up that the check was no good. Not to mention that I would have apologized and offered to pay any charges that the overdraft caused, which he never did.

His true colors have shown, as he has conveniently not had the time or money to show up for most family events over the last several years, disappointing many in our small family.

It also frustrated me that one of my uncle's favorite things was to change the terms of our agreement, even those that were in writing. He always said he wasn't counting my money and would then point out that I didn't actually need the money. Then he would quickly add that he was family. Believe me, the terms we agreed on in the first place were for people who had an "A" credit rating, which he absolutely didn't.

When you buy a franchise like an IHOP they require that you have a certain net worth. Of course my uncle was always a country mile from what he called the "ridiculous standard" that IHOP imposes. Why would you need to have a reserve when you are buying such a great business? Don't get me wrong, my uncle is hard-working and a pretty good business operator. That said, he seems to walk around with a black cloud over him. If something could go wrong, like a sewer backing up, or equipment lasting for a shorter time than its expected life, or a clause in a contract that is misinterpreted actually mattering, it would definitely go wrong. Murphy's Law was written based on guys like him.

One of the first things they teach you in business school is that many businesses have failed because they aren't well capitalized. That is unless your nephew is Mitchell Epstein. Then you play the "I'm going to lose everything" card. Each time he needed money, the story was always that either he wouldn't be able to buy the business, or he was at risk of losing everything and there was nowhere else to turn. As I said, not exactly the characteristics of an "A" credit rating.

Since this book includes the good, the bad, and the ugly, I will reluctantly admit that I not only lent my uncle money to buy one IHOP, but I made the mistake twice! You are probably wondering how in the world he convinced me the second time. He had an opportunity to buy a second IHOP, and I of course was the only one able to help him with this life-changing opportunity! Recognizing that I was not happy with how things were going with the first deal and that I had no interest in "helping him out" again, he quickly changed his pitch.

He presented this as a business opportunity, and we structured a deal that was good for both of us. Can you guess what happened? Of course, less than a year later he changed the deal on me. What was I going to do – sue my uncle? Fool me once, shame on you; fool me twice –WOW! I am not sure what the life lesson is here, except not to lend money to family. I think it's safe to say my mother was right about not getting involved financially with her ex-brother-in-law.

In full disclosure, my uncle has eventually made all of his payments under the revised terms. Just recently, after thirteen years, he sold his first store, and I'm now off the hook as the full guarantor of that IHOP. Although he still owes me money, he has told me that I just need to be patient and he assures me that I won't lose a dime.

How is our relationship today? We have minimal contact, as our phone calls usually frustrate or disappoint me. Additionally, as I said, he rarely shows up to family events so we haven't had an opportunity to visit in a setting where I might see him in the light that I once did.

What would have happened if I'd just said no to his first request? Who can say, but how could that have been worse? I have little respect for him now, and I'm sad to say I lost a relationship with someone I once looked up to and loved very much.

The Right Way to Do Things

A couple of years after we moved to Sarasota, a friend of Dawn's was going through a nasty divorce. She hadn't worked in years and wasn't the most financially astute person. Like too many women she had not been actively involved in managing and monitoring her finances, as she had trusted her husband. As the dust settled, she found out they either didn't have any assets or that her husband had hidden them. This included the house they had lived in. Worse yet, her husband had destroyed her credit.

This woman was the opposite of lucky. On paper her situation was bleak. But she had something more powerful than money – a positive attitude. She was determined to bounce back, and she was looking to buy a house for her and her daughter. She had the courage to ask my wife if we would help her.

I met with her and listened to her story, which was heartbreaking to say the least. On the bright side, she had found a house that cost $112,000 and somehow managed to come up with about $12,000. The house needed a new roof, and she had already lined up someone to do the work for $9,500. Her problem was that there was obviously no way she would qualify for a traditional loan. She asked if we could help her until she cleared up her credit, which she thought would take three years.

Dawn and I have been so fortunate in our lives, financially and otherwise, and we feel that giving back is paramount. At the same time, we worked extremely hard for everything we have, so it's crucial to me that our money actually helps somebody rather than just lets them off the hook. We felt that this was a scenario where it made sense to take a chance on someone. I put together a rent-to-own lease based on her initial $12,000 payment and included an additional $100 a month toward her purchase price, assuming that she made her monthly payments. Then we crossed our fingers.

Each month for five years her payment arrived on time. I think there was one month when she called and asked if it would be a problem if she was a day or two late. Some months she would drop off a check at our house on the day that it was due to avoid being late.

How did she manage to do this? Simple: She busted her ass, just as we had. She worked two jobs, and in each case she started out in an entry-level position. During those five years she also managed to do various fixer-upper projects on her house. I'm so happy to say that when she refinanced her house last year to pay us off, the house was appraised for a little over $200,000, meaning she had approximately $90,000 in equity.

I'm sure that nothing was easy for her during those five years. She was a single mom, working two jobs, but she didn't let an exceptionally difficult situation stop her. During each step of the five-year process, whether it was fixing the roof, landscaping, building a deck, and finally qualifying for a mortgage, she rolled up her sleeves and researched what needed to be done. Then she found a way to do each of these things.

She inspired me, and I hope her grit and determination inspire you. She is a true example of a Ms. Lucky: focused on the bright side, hard-working, honest, grateful, and persistent. She created her own luck and raised a wonderful daughter. I have all the respect in the world for her!

Life Lessons from Mr. Lucky

Most people lose money when they gamble.

Don't take money for granted.

Don't count other people's money.

Lending money to family and friends risks a lot more than money.

Do unto others as you would have them do unto you.

A positive attitude will take you a long way.

CHAPTER 30
Temple Youth Group

One fall day in 2008, my daughter surprised us by saying that she wanted to go to a Temple Youth Group meeting; she had heard they were fun and hoped to meet people. As Dawn was dropping off Mel, she went in and met Dan, the dad of another participant. He asked Dawn where she was from and a little about herself. He pointed out his wife Debbie and introduced the two of them, saying that they had so much in common, including both of them being artists from Atlanta.

That night proved to be memorable, as Dawn and Debbie started a deep friendship that has since expanded to include both of our families. Equally exciting, Mel made some friends and decided to join the Youth Group.

What made this so unexpected was that after her Bat Mitzvah, which I forced upon her, she had no interest in being involved with temple. Not only did she join the Youth Group, but she ended up attending the temple's confirmation class and getting confirmed when she turned sixteen. She was also on the board of her Youth Group and traveled to many weekend events with them, rarely missing one.

The Youth Group was fantastic in so many ways, due in no small part to their energetic and supportive leader, Andrea Eiffert. The Youth Group provided numerous opportunities each year to go on trips and participate in both Jewish services and activities with other Jewish students. Even though my wife and I are not religious, making sure Mel had exposure to other Jewish children and learned about our heritage was very important, especially to me.

Figure Out What Matters to You

I was raised Jewish and had a Bar Mitzvah when I was thirteen years old. Dawn is Jewish but her family wasn't religious and didn't observe or celebrate Jewish holidays. I was the first Jew that Dawn dated (at twenty-seven years old), and I wanted to raise our child as a Jew. This was never an issue except when the time came for Mel to begin the process of studying for her Bat Mitzvah.

Like many eleven-year-olds, Mel was not interested in studying for a Bat Mitzvah. Dawn and I had a lot of discussion about this, and her opinion was that we shouldn't make Mel do it. I almost gave in, but when I asked my mother for guidance, she strongly encouraged me to insist on the Bat Mitzvah. She reasoned that given the history of the Jews, particularly the killing of six million people in the Holocaust, having knowledge of our heritage was essential.

I'm glad that I held my ground, and I believe we are all happy that Mel had a Bat Mitzvah. Most people don't realize how intense the Bar/Bat Mitzvah process is until you point out that a twelve-year-old has to learn a language that uses completely unfamiliar symbols and is essentially written backwards, as the letters go from right to left. If that isn't difficult enough, the most significant portion of the service involves reading from the Torah, which doesn't have any vowels. I'm proud to say that Mel did a terrific job.

Learn About Your Heritage

None of us would realize how impactful the Bat Mitzvah decision was until years later, when each of us went to Israel. Jewish teens and adults up to thirty-two years old are provided an essentially free trip to Israel called "Birthright," which Melanie did when she was nineteen. Dawn and I finally traveled to Israel two years ago, when we were fifty-seven.

Our trip to Israel was the most meaningful of our life. We have been fortunate to have the opportunity to travel more than most, so I would be hard-pressed to explain why it took me fifty-seven years to go to Israel. Thankfully our good friend – the youth group leader who now works for the Jewish Federation of Sarasota – approached us about putting together a trip for a group of friends. Fourteen of us went on this fabulous ten-day tour.

Our knowledgeable guide, Shachar Gal, took us to the typical places, like the heartbreaking Yad Vashem (the World Holocaust Remembrance Center); the breathtaking Masada; the holiest of holy places, the Wailing Wall; and of course we floated in the Dead Sea. These experiences alone would have made for a fantastic trip, but we also had an engrossing Jeep tour in the Upper Galilee with a brigadier general, the former director for Counterterrorism; a riveting two-hour lunch at Mt. Bental on the Syrian border with an Israeli general; and an enlightening GeoPolitical tour with Israeli Colonel Danny Tirza, who was responsible for planning the security fence between Israel and the West Bank.

This portion of the trip was the most engrossing history, religion, and politics lesson of our lives. What made it so impactful was that it was about our people. What the Israelis have made out of a desert and accomplished in just seventy years is phenomenal. What we have overcome as a people is astounding. I never felt so proud to be a Jew.

The learning never ended, even during the "just for fun" portion of the trip. We hiked the beautiful Ein Gedi Reserve and the even more breathtaking Banias Falls, and took a cable car to Rosh Hanikrah, where we saw spectacular grottos. Our group was also treated to a delicious dinner at the home of an Israeli chef; we browsed and purchased unique jewelry and art in a magnificent artist market in Safed; and experienced a fascinating graffiti walking tour in the Tel Aviv neighborhood of Florentin. The mostly healthy and always tasty culinary experiences throughout Israel included a market tour in Tel Aviv and tastings at two wineries in the Golan Heights.

The food, wine, and beauty of Israel alone would be worthy of a visit for anyone, and frankly that's what most of our vacations are about. There is no doubt that the world has many places rich in history, including here in the United States. That said, I have never been on a trip where I interacted with two generals and a colonel, had a tour guide so knowledgeable about Jewish and Israeli history, culture, and politics, and learned so much in such an enjoyable way.

Sadly, the antisemitism that Jews still face in most parts of the world is horrendous. I don't believe this is the right forum to defend the humanitarian efforts of the Jews or say much about the thousands of life-changing scientific discoveries, technological achievements, and medical breakthroughs of Israelis. However, I will quickly and proudly state that as of 2017, there have been 892 Nobel Prizes awarded to individuals; 201 of them have been awarded to Jews. It's amazing that a group of people that represents 0.2 percent of the world's population makes up 22.5 percent of Nobel Prize recipients.

Life Lessons from Mr. Lucky

Learning about your heritage is very powerful.

Sometimes you have to make your kids do something.

CHAPTER 31
Hit the Road, Jack

During the twenty-five years that I traveled for business, I spent time in many small towns and rural places. I know I'm going to overgeneralize and likely piss off many friends and family, because there are obviously warm and friendly people everywhere. However, these people were much friendlier and more relaxed, compared with those in the big northeastern cities. I often traveled alone and used to joke that in the Midwest they would always invite you to dinner and sometimes it would include their families. In the Northeast, you were lucky if they took the time to recommend a good place for you to eat.

In my earlier days of business travel, before I owned US Banking Alliance, I would go to minor league baseball games whenever I could. The stadiums are relatively small so I always had a good seat, and there was something exciting about the hustle from players trying to make it to the big leagues. And a beer doesn't cost $12 at a minor league game. When I was really lucky, I would be in a college town during basketball season. I even had the opportunity to see a couple of Gator games while traveling for business.

I encourage everyone to travel as often as possible. There are hundreds of wonderful trips for every budget all over the world, as well as in our beautiful country, offering an endless array of varied opportunities. Walking barefoot on the beach with the sights, sounds, and smell of the water is peaceful, calming, and rejuvenating. If that doesn't do it for you, try one of our majestic national parks – they are true treasures. The cost for a carload of people to visit Yellowstone National Park is $35 for an entire week.

One of the reasons Dawn and I travel is we love to meet people from different cultures. When you are traveling this happens so naturally, whether you are sitting at a café or looking at a pretty sight. It's an opportunity to get a completely different perspective about anything and everything. There is no better way to gain a greater understanding of the world than by meeting with, and talking to, a diverse group of people.

Our passion for wine and travel exposes us to a lot more than just the "good stuff" as there is poverty virtually everywhere. Two meaningful examples are Amani Children's Home in Moshi, Tanzania and the V Foundation. Amani was started by part-time Sarasota residents Beverly and Tom Porter to rescue homeless children from the streets and provide shelter, food, and education. The Porters are the proprietors of Porter Family Vineyards, an absolutely beautiful winery producing small quantities of delicious wine in Napa Valley.

One of Sarasota's most famous residents is Dick Vitale. He and his wife Lorraine devote endless hours supporting pediatric cancer research as part of the V Foundation he helped start for his friend Jimmy Valvano. Their Wine Celebration is one of the most delectable ways to raise money for cancer research.

Dawn and I are usually able to incorporate winery visits into our travel. We always enjoy meeting the winemakers and vineyard owners, and hearing them speak so passionately about their journey. Years later we can still feel their emotion as we drink the delicious juice they so lovingly made. In addition to the captivating stories and fabulous wine, the views from each winery seem more gorgeous than the last. Occasionally in Italy we had a tour or tasting with someone who didn't speak English, but somehow we all managed to communicate through the magic of the wine.

On one of our first trips to Tuscany, we were driving along and I noticed the sign at the entrance to Ciacci Piccolomini, a winery we love and that I highly recommend. They make a couple of magnificent Brunello di Montalcinos, which are reasonably priced, and their simple, low-cost Rosso di Montalcino and Ateo are enjoyable, vintage after vintage (year after year).

I knocked on the door and was pleasantly surprised when someone answered. I explained that I had written ahead and knew they were closed, but that they were our absolute favorite Italian winery and I just couldn't drive by without stopping. The owner, Paolo Bianchini, graciously gave us a forty-five-minute tour. Although we didn't taste any wine that day, we took pictures with him and his sister (she's the co-owner), and they gave each of us a beautiful long-sleeve, button-down shirt with their logo.

My persistence paid off and his generosity did as well, since we currently have about 125 bottles of their wine in our cellar, and I have probably purchased and enjoyed another three hundred over the years.

Life Lessons from Mr. Lucky

Traveling has many great benefits.

There are great trips for every budget.

CONCLUSION

I did it, I wrote a book. My hope is that you have found reading it much easier than I found writing it. More important is my hope that you feel more prepared to deal with life's challenges and inspired to help yourself and others achieve their goals and dreams. Why not? If I can write a book, there is almost nothing you can't do if you set your mind to it.

When I told people that I only had to write the conclusion to complete my manuscript, each one of them immediately congratulated me. I thanked them but at first didn't quite recognize and appreciate the significance of this project. As I reflect back, the eighteen-month journey was full of Mr. Lucky moments. The process of writing this book really had two segments: the process aspect and the spiritual part.

First, the process. I had absolutely no idea how to write a book. Like most of us learning something new, I began with a quick internet search and a "how hard can it be?" attitude. I found an exhaustive number of articles, seminars, and books about writing a book. I quickly read two articles and was overwhelmed with all the advice. I decided that my hard work, stick-to-itiveness, and common sense would guide me through this process, just as it had most everything in my life.

I knew one thing for sure. In order to write a book I actually had to start writing. That is to say, I needed to put words on a page; and so I began. No outline, no organization, frankly no nothing. In hindsight, I admit that there are definitely better ways.

Still, I loved the process. I sat down at the computer and wrote about whatever topic I had chosen for however long I decided. I constantly reminded myself that my objective was to help others. In fact, every dollar I receive from this project will go to nonprofits supporting children's causes and education.

The most valuable part of the process was the spiritual aspect. I was able to relive most of my life. I got to think about, explore, and *feel* the life that I had blown right through. It was difficult, and I was constantly challenged to go deeper.

The first person who challenged me to go inside further was Patricia O'Connell, a *New York Times* best-selling author whom I randomly met at PrecisionLender's Bank on Purpose conference. We were at the welcome party, and I asked her why she was attending. She replied that she was there to make a presentation, "Win More Customers," based on her book. She also told me that she had been an editor at *Business Week* magazine and helped other authors.

At this point I was about six months into the project and hadn't told more than a few people that I was writing a book. My biggest question at the time was, "Do I really have something that could actually be a book?" I knew I was benefitting from being so reflective, but if I was only writing for myself, I could get the words on paper without worrying about all the literary elements that I knew so little about.

Patricia offered to read the first chunk, and I waited with bated breath for her feedback. Finally an email arrived saying she thought I had something. "Your story IS inspirational, and you have some trenchant insights and some 'tough love' to give – sometimes more tough; sometimes more love." Admittedly I had to look up the definition of trenchant and laughed to myself that probably no one will need a dictionary to read my book.

She also said I had to give more, a lot more, and go much deeper. After we agreed to work together she kept pushing, asking, "What else were you feeling? How did this affect your feelings about family, money, obligation, etc.?" This inner inquisition was extremely uncomfortable but I pushed through, hopefully making the book more valuable to both you and me.

Each time Patricia's feedback would arrive, I would think about the training experience with my best friend Courtney. I think there were times that Patricia provided no positive feedback, just enumerated everything that needed to be done better. I was sure that I had at least used the shiiit sandwich approach with Courtney: You start with something positive, then list the endless number of ways you could do better, followed with something positive. Patricia served me only the middle of the sandwich and it sure didn't taste good.

I would have to give myself a Mr. Lucky pep talk each time. "Do you want her to say nice stuff, or do you want her to help you write a book that motivates people?" I would ask myself. How many meetings had I had with my sales guy, John, and others throughout my career, and my life, where I had been brutally honest, with little concern for anything more than achieving a desired result? I certainly hadn't worried about the emotional impact of my words. With hindsight being 20-20, I think I could have been as effective with words that were just as direct but a little gentler. Perhaps in some cases we might even have accomplished more.

So many others showed up at just the right time to help me take the project up a notch. For example, this past Christmas Eve as I was coming down the home stretch with the book, Dawn and I went to a special yoga class. I was waiting for her after class when a sweet lady whom I had met but never spoken with asked what I do. For one of the first times in my life, I answered that I was writing a book. She told me she had written and published three books. We met and she put me in touch with an editor who once again challenged me.

Of course the road to completion also included life's little challenges. For example, early in the process I brought my iPad instead of a laptop so I could work on the book while I was out of town. I lost, and never was able to locate, the file containing what were no doubt award-winning passages. Moments like this are almost always still challenging; however, they remind us of what is really important. No one died and no one was diagnosed with a heartbreaking disease. I have to be content with the fact that I am now much more aware of my feelings in the moment.

In closing, aside from convincing everyone to give yoga a try, I hope after reading this book you believe that the world is full of people who would love to help you; who truly "Do unto others" and who live life from the heart. If your life is already fantastic, I congratulate you and wish you the best going forward. I also challenge you to give back. If you need help, don't be afraid to ask for it. Most importantly, when you see others who do, ask them if they would like your assistance. Whether you call it kindness, compassion, self-lessness, or service – it's all love.

Postscript: Jeron just left my house after telling me he is going to be able to graduate six months earlier than he thought. Wow; he has been going to school and working full time since we met over five years ago. I couldn't be happier for him, or more thankful for the opportunity to mentor him and Coy; it's so unbelievably rewarding.

Finally, I thank you for your time and simply say: Peace to all, love to all, may you see the light, and be the light to help make the world a better place.

ACKNOWLEDGMENTS

I am beyond grateful to all who supported me through what was perhaps the most unexpected part of my life journey: writing a book. I have never received more help with an initiative in my life than I did with this one.

To say that my wife Dawn encouraged me from beginning to end would be a humongous understatement. She patiently read each draft, providing valuable input, edits, and recollections of our life. Not once did she point out or make me feel worse about my many character flaws as I became more aware about the person I was and have become.

Dawn lifted me up each time I received valuable input from others that knocked my fragile male ego for a loop. And of course I am forever grateful that she woke up in the middle of the night to save our family from a raging house fire. Having her by my side is the truest reflection of why I am, without a doubt, Mr. Lucky.

Coy Carter and Jeron Thomas are an important part of my life. The joy and satisfaction I receive from our relationships inspired me to write this book. They are both amazing individuals. I love them and look forward to continuing to share our lives.

Ken Garcia, a co-founder at PrecisionLender and friend, was the first person with whom I shared an early passage from the book. His gentle but very clear feedback let me know that not only was I missing the mark, but I wasn't even close. Most important, though, were his encouragement and suggestions for what needed to be done.

Patricia O'Connell contributed to the book by not only helping me to examine my words, but also the deeper meaning of my life. I described her key role in the process more fully in the book's conclusion.

I was especially pleased that my daughter Melanie enjoyed reading the book and gaining a greater understanding about me. She patiently pointed out that way too many sentences began with the words "And," "Or", or "But". Even more importantly, I hope she knows how proud I am that she is my daughter and how much I love her.

Gari Carter is a very inspiring individual. I benefited from my chance meeting with her after yoga class.

Stacey, Maddie, and Sammie (my fantastic cousins who read multiple drafts of the book) contributed significantly with their kind words, encouragement, and direction. Thankfully they stood firm when I pushed back.

Carol Gaskin, my second editor, helped me to organize my unstructured text and create something I am proud to share with the world.

I am very appreciative for the encouragement and suggestions my sister Lisa Ferraro provided. She is absolutely the best sister in the world.

Carrie Silverstein, a wonderfully joyful friend whom I have known since college, when she started dating (and subsequently married) my good friend Richard Silverstein, provided some timely advice and encouragement as I headed into the home stretch.

My goddaughter Julia Ferraro not only provided me with valuable feedback during the editing process, but created the book cover. She is as talented and wonderful as her beautiful cover. I am so proud to have her work introducing my book.

Aunt Marilyn, Uncle Richard, Cousin Beth, and her husband Rob all not only took the time to read the book but spent hours providing me with countless ways to enhance the reader experience.

I can't thank my mother enough. Let's face it, there is no job in the world that is more important, challenging, and underappreciated than being a mother. And she has been a great mother. My mom's first words and tone of voice, "Why would you want to do that?" when I told her that I was writing this book, inspired me to make it the best I could. And her email after reading the book that stated that she was overwhelmed with pride and thought the book was amazing brought tears to my eyes.

Finally, a big thank you to everyone along the way who said they were excited to read my book. Those simple words meant so much to me. I have been Mr. Lucky time and again for having known you all.